Manipulation
and
Dark Psychology

The complete guide to learn to understand, recognize, and contrast the effects of mental manipulation and of the dark psychology.

Thom Janson

TABLE OF CONTENTS

Manipulation and Dark Psychology

INTRODUCTION

Bad things happen to good people. Do they though? What if there was a way to take control of situations and successfully position ourselves in the driver's seat? You are confronted every day with persuasion, manipulation, and dark psychology through TV ads, social media, and everyday conversations with friends and loved ones. Are you handling these interactions the best way you can? If you feel that you are not in control of these interactions, or feel outmatched in negotiating your position in situations, this book could provide you the leverage in gaining a better understanding of the power struggle that evolves in every relationship that you have.

This book provides insight into the world of sinister behavior in human relationships and gives you the tools to rise from those shadows. Understanding why people act the way they do, and why you behave as you do, is a large piece of the puzzle to change the relationship. Understanding how the mind works and how emotions are tools to benefit another is critical in realizing where you fit into these relationships and how to transition from unwilling victim to self-reliant individual.

Learning the psychology behind interactions with other people is an essential prelude to controlling the outcome for different results. This book offers guidance to avoid predatory people and relationships. It also provides guidance to navigate those relationships or end them. This book will delve into the world of dark manipulation and how predators use it to get what they want and how you can avoid these situations, or better yet, control them.

This book discusses the benefits of knowing your psyche and how to improve emotional intelligence skills to succeed in all aspects of your life. Emotional intelligence plays an essential role in self-discovery and being able to read and navigate life's situations. Practical navigation skills give you the strength to identify relationships that you may need to reevaluate or dismiss.

The primary way to change your circumstance in life is to understand people and their intentions. People greet us every day, whether online or in-person. To have an intimate understanding of what motivates them allows you to develop the quality of life that you seek; it is vital to have the knowledge and tools to elevate your situation.

In taking a walk on the dark side, we can discover what motivates people, and businesses, for that matter, to take advantage of others and what weapons we can put in our arsenal to prevent these situations both in our careers and personal lives. It is imperative to strengthen your social skills, identify problems, and find that superpower within yourself to know, with absolute confidence, that you got this.

The goal is, after reading this book, you can identify dark traits in specific situations. You will be able to read people correctly and amplify the good qualities within yourself to protect your mind from being maliciously invaded while simultaneously giving you the power to acquire and sustain a satisfaction with your life in career, relationship, home, and community.

CHAPTER 1: THE ARTS OF PERSUASION AND MANIPULATION

The conversation took place sitting at the Cadillac dealership in a new Cadillac Escalade. The fresh car smell was intoxicating, and as the lumbar rollers laid their magic on my back, I turned my head to my spouse and thought, *how do I get this car.* As my eyes narrowed for battle, my opponent leaned back in the chair, preparing the counter strike. The simple truth was that we could not afford this car. The overwhelming fact was that my want for convenience and luxury overwhelmed any simple, common-sense reality.

The dual began with us exchanging practical facts about why and why not. I realized I would not win this argument on points and opted for the convenience and quality of life angle, thus promptly refuting useful facts in ninja-like speed. Rethinking my strategy, I briefly considered prompting a few not so veiled ultimatums before kicking my impractical brat to the curb and letting the adult in me resurface to agree with my adversary that yes, we could not afford the car. The practical side was trumping my impractical side. Yay, go me!

Now, the question becomes, was I using persuasion to win my argument, or was I tapping the manipulation button? Was my significant other using persuasion, manipulation, both, or neither? The boundaries become a bit blurred in the heat of the moment, but there is a fine line between persuasion and manipulation. This line will be highlighted, bolded, and set in neon in this Chapter to be easily defined and identified. You will successfully determine what is persuasion and what is manipulation and have the tools to navigate both.

Persuasion

There have been several books published that provide various definitions for what persuasion is. A persuasion is a tool wielded by people to influence thoughts and behavior. You find persuasion in business, social media, advertisements, casual gaming, parenting, and nearly all activity that requires any type of interaction or conversation.

In today's society, Social Influencers make millions with a straightforward task – to influence what you buy. They climb the ranks of the social ladder, and if they are outstanding, they have millions of followers. They know their audience and so do Companies. Companies will reach out to Social Influencers in attempts to get them to co-sign their products. In doing so, the Companies stand to gain increased revenue, and the Social Influencer stands to profit.

This influence can be subtle, like wearing a designer jacket and not saying a word about it on their YouTube post. Or, it could be bolder, like the Influencer holding up the book they just 'bought' and saying it changed their life. Social media is fast and finite. Things happen instantly, and trends fly like wildfire. Adverting in social media is just one example that you encounter every day.

Every one of us has a belief system or opinion. Someone with strong convictions may have the language skills to communicate their ideas in such a way to influence others to change their attitudes or behaviors to align better with their beliefs. Attorneys are trained in such skills and negotiations, as are politicians. Politicians are extraordinary in this skillset. They address the public daily to convince you of why you should or should not believe this or that. It is an acquired skill. The element of persuasion is essential for public speakers, like attorneys and politicians, but it is equally valuable to the ordinary individual in everyday conversations.

The Four Modes of Persuasion

Aristotle coined the four critical modes of persuasion that still hold today, although found in several more mediums than the ancient Greeks ever thought possible. Aristotle defined these modes as Ethos, Pathos, Logos, and Kairos. To persuade successfully, the greater the presence of these four elements, the more likely it is to sway someone towards your position.

<u>Ethos means character</u>. Trust is of profound importance in one's ability to persuade another. If you think about it, it makes perfect sense. If the speaker is a reliable member of your circle of trust, you highly value their opinion. If it is someone you don't know, you evaluate their merit by measuring personal experience or known authority and then decide if you can trust them or not. The greater the level of trust, the more you will have faith that their argument is sound, and the less guarded you will be to hear their views.

This trust is tested and applied to any medium. What this means is whether it is written or spoken, we look to that person's authority in the form of experience, influence, education, qualifications, invested interest in their audience, or accomplishments. One could call it analyzing their 'trust resume' and weighing whether it resonates with you as satisfactory or not.

<u>Pathos means suffering, experience, or emotion</u>. We all can relate to the human condition, root for the underdog, and find inspiration in overcoming hardship. Stories are what engage us and stimulate our minds far more than reciting facts. We want to empathize, to share experiences, to relate with heart-

wrenching compassion. Humans are social creatures and crave interaction, making us all closet romantics.

Pathos in a communicator can tap into the vein of our emotions and pull out relatable experiences that help build trust. Giving good Pathos translates to the audience being able to identify with the communicator and understanding their position. Effective communication is a direct path to having an open-minded conversation and giving a little of ourselves in each direction. Many arguments have been won without facts and instead have won on appealing to our emotions. The heart usually wins over the head.

<u>Logos means word or reason</u>. This one goes out to the head over the heart population. Some people need the facts and figures of things. For some of us to consider changing our minds, we require a sound argument for any level of persuasion to gain momentum. Logos is when you can quote outside sources and present well-known or proven concrete facts. There is no grey area here. There are no romancing words. These are facts known to be truths, and the communicator is well versed in them.

Facts must come from an area of expertise, a proven track record of accomplishment and study, authoritative sources, or scientific proof. If the communicator has these to bolster their argument, they could effectively win on Logos alone. However, it's not very fun. Remember the Escalade argument from earlier? Enough said.

<u>Kairos means qualitative time.</u> You will find this type of persuasion abundant in advertising. Kairos creates a sense of urgency or an act now kind of feeling. Don't let this offer pass by. Hurry before it's too late. Kairos can also be in the timing of a good joke, and some are just too soon or far too late. Kairos usually doesn't come into play in everyday conversations with friends or colleagues unless you argue about the benefits of a destination while sitting in a taxi with the meter running; however, Kairos is just as vital as the other three modes in persuasion.

Now that you understand how people utilize the power of persuasion, there is one significant thought that should be playing amplified in your head before engaging. The defining note about persuasion is both you and the communicator act in confidence that the exchange is voluntary. You both remain in the safe harbor to disagree and maintain your own beliefs. If the conversation feels mutual rather than forced, it is a huge indicator that the exchange is voluntary, and there is free-will.

An Important Defining Note About Persuasion

A critical element that occurs in the art of persuasion is the communication of the message. It is essential to know what the intent is behind the message. During the communication exchange, persuasion is exercised equally by both sides. What this means is, all people involved are contributing to the conversation with what they believe to be the truth, and do not feel coerced. They can make up their mind on whether or not they change their belief on a topic or action without fear of consequences from the other party.

A good rule to live by while using persuasion tactics in a conversation is to give the audience substance, like food for thought. Give them time to chew the meat, savor it, and give their critique before swallowing it. Then provide them with the space to decide whether or not they like the taste. A good persuasion chef allows time for the topic to simmer because the intent is to enlighten, to learn, to find common ground, and satisfy social cravings of interaction. Persuasion is not about forcibly thrusting your idea upon others and coercing their behavior to do something against their better judgment. Persuasion leads to better understanding. Knowledge is power in making better choices that make you feel good. Persuasion leaves someone in a better place than when you found them.

Techniques & Uses of Persuasion

As you have realized by now, we are confronted with persuasion every day. Not just confronted, a better word may be 'overwhelmed.' Some influence is so subtle it goes undetected. Others provide such a sense of urgency that you just have to get that item before its gone – as in sales pitches. Social media has opened the door to the availability of persuasion that enters our daily lives. There are several techniques.

1. <u>Get it now! It Won't Last!</u> (Scarcity)– You have probably heard this quite frequently on the radio of your car, your phone, or TV. The limited-time offers are persuading you to get up off your seat and into the store. This technique refers to the scarcity principle. Don't miss your opportunity.

2. <u>I rub your back, and you scratch mine</u>. (Reciprocity)– If someone does you a favor, you feel obligated to return it. This sense of obligation is known as the Reciprocity Norm. The persuasion plays upon the good samaritan in you to return the favor.

3. <u>If 4 out of 5 doctors recommend this product, they must be right.</u> (Authority) – Relying on the authority of others' opinions may sway your opinion. If professionals are all in agreement, the

product must be good, and therefore I must run out and buy it.

4. <u>Everybody is doing it</u>. (Conversion)– Well, if everyone is doing it, maybe I should too. The majority in a position can often change your stance on things because it is a popular opinion. The words from your mom, "If Johnny jumped off a cliff, would you do it too?". Are swiftly forgotten in the presence of a mob in favor of something. Majority rules are known as the Conversion Theory.

5. <u>I am 100% sure!</u> (Amplification)– If the speaker is communicating a topic that you are not 100% sure about, and they speak with such certainty and conviction, that may be enough to persuade you to their line of thinking. This uncertainty is the Amplification Theory.

6. <u>I can't get that commercial jingle out of my head</u>. (Priming)– Bringing something up repeatedly in different situations and conversations is priming you to change your mind and is near-subliminal messaging. Have you ever eaten something and were unsure if you liked it or not, but then people keep saying how great it was at different social gatherings that you attend? So, the natural thing to do is order it again? Same principle. It's subtle and persuasive.

There are other techniques and theories, but these are the primary ones introduced into our lives daily and show how these persuasion tools work. Successful persuasion is why successful advertisers make the big bucks. Having advertising that starts a trend or influences the masses comes with a high price tag because it is a coveted, cutthroat market.

Studies on buyer behavior identify what you have done or what you are likely to do. Buyer behavior is when you are looking on FaceBook, and an ad pops up for what a friend purchased, so you take a look at it and buy one yourself. This pings over to analytics and gives them the insight that you like that kind of product. This ping tells them to offer more related products to you as you may purchase them. Analytics are studied and reported so companies can develop custom advertising. Custom advertising is valuable to Companies because they can hit their target audience more effectively. After all, there are nearly as many people online as there are on earth.

Manipulation

The word manipulation carries a stigma with it, which is well earned. Manipulation separates itself from persuasion because manipulation by the communicator exerts dominance through their influence over the communicatee. The intent is to take power away from someone for one's benefit by exploiting that person's emotions or convoluting facts as an act of deception.

Some manipulation can be subtle and sneak up on you, while other forms are so abrupt that it takes you off guard, and you go along to get along. It is essential to understand the different types of manipulation, and how they are used, so you don't fall victim and have the means to take power back. Manipulation is the staple in toxic relationships. Now, keep in mind there are levels of manipulation. Not all manipulation is that vile or sinister. Think back on something that you wanted, say like, an Escalade. Small manipulations take place every day; it does not mean that people are evil. A bit of history in actions and intents are required to understand if you are being manipulated comprehensively.

Remember how we discussed Ethos (character) and Pathos (emotions)? Manipulation usually always works because the person that is using the weapon of manipulation is one of authority or emotionally connected to you. This person is in your circle of trust. It is when the member is in the circle of trust that the line blurs. You believe in your heart that this person has your best interest in mind. This kind of manipulation sneaks up on you, or you are aware that it is happening but lack the skills to flip the script, or you may be in absolute denial in your urge to avoid conflict.

Manipulation presented to you by strangers is far easier to identify and to reject. The Ethos is lacking or absent, so their words or actions do not hold as much weight with you. Some people have mastered manipulation so well that it has become a lucrative full-time job. Manipulation takes the four modes of persuasion and perverts them with wicked intent and pretense. There are still darker things that we encounter every day that deserve mention.

Introduction to Dark Psychology

Are we born good or evil? It is an age-old question that has been under debate since the words first escaped lips. If we turn back to knowledgeable old Aristotle, he believed we are born amoral and learn morality if someone guides us. If we do not have guidance, we stay with our amoral ways. Although the argument may be far from settled, there is one thing that most fields of study can agree on: Humans are capable of great atrocities in both behavior and action.

Dark Psychology digs into that world by examining the psychological nature as to why certain people prey on others and how they do it. Criminal tendencies are prevalent in a portion of the population. The same moral boundaries do not restrain this set of the community as others. The main tools of those with certain traits are various forms of manipulation. We will touch more on dark psychology later in this book, but it required an introduction here as manipulation plays a massive role in operating.

Covert Manipulation

Covert manipulation can is defined as attacking a person's self-worth and lowering their confidence and value to the point they place their well-being in the attacker's hands. The attacker continues to hack away at their self-esteem and self-worth until there is nothing left and renders the victim utterly co-dependent with all of the control given to the attacker.

This type of manipulation, breaking apart another person is dangerous and is done by the most insidious of manipulators, including psychopaths and narcissists. Both consider themselves shepherds among sheep and have no moral compass that says it is wrong to prey on others.

Covert manipulation starts with a great deal of affection to coax you into their grip. It is similar to how predators in the wild hunt their prey. It is how easily they insert themselves into your life and make it remarkable that it is disorienting as they begin to take it away. You end up wondering what you did wrong because, indeed, they wouldn't be treating you this way unless…you deserved it? You must know manipulation techniques to see the signs of being manipulated. If you can see it coming, you can learn how to turn it around or entirely avoid the situation.

Techniques & Signs of Manipulation

As with persuasion, there are several techniques used in manipulation. They are more subtle and usually require a great deal of time because they mask their intent. Most people do not even realize that they have been manipulated. They are surprised by the direct conflict with their emotional connection to the person.   There are some standard techniques that you should be aware of:

1. <u>Master instigators</u>. Manipulators come into their power over someone by splitting them away from the herd. The easiest way to do this is by causing a fight or hard feelings between the person they want to manipulate and their closest connections. The goal for a manipulator is to have their target dependent on them. It is far easier to control the victim if there are less caring people to look out for them. If the manipulator can sever those ties, all the better for him.

2. <u>Hot & Cold</u>. Manipulators get the victim dependent and in compliance by rewarding the victim with their presence, but on their terms. When the victim needs

them, the manipulator will pull away. This distance reinforces how much the victim feels they need the manipulator. The silent absence of the manipulator's presence when the victim needs them is loud, especially if the manipulator has successfully severed the victim's relationship ties to others that would have been there. That is why there are good days and bad days; expect a lot of these. It is conditional control.

3. <u>Attacking the victim's self-worth</u>. Manipulators will exert dominance over the victim by taking their self-esteem down to a nub. The manipulator gets the victim to question their self-worth and doubt what they are capable of doing. As self-worth whittles away, the victim continues to surrender any control over their lives and feelings to the manipulator. It's the dependency on the manipulator that gives them power over the victim. Every action the manipulator takes is to seize that power and maintain it. It is the ultimate chess game with many moving parts playing at once. They are orchestrated and well-thought-out.

There are specific ways in which manipulators take a victim's self-esteem, which will be addressed later in this book. These three techniques are based on what a manipulator's goal is, and you should be aware of them.

Differences Between Persuasion & Manipulation

We have defined persuasion and manipulation in great detail. Some key differences immediately noticed between the two.

Persuasion focuses on the exchange of ideas and free-will. Manipulation focuses on an imbalance of power and forced-will.

Trust is the main ingredient in both. Can you trust this person? Does this person have your best interest at heart? Do you feel better when you are around this person, or do you breathe more freely away from them?

These are questions you need to ask yourself if you start to question the intentions of someone that you are close to or work with daily. Now that you know these differences, you may need to reevaluate some exchanges that you have participated in with other people. Maybe you need to rethink some relationships. If you are asking yourself how you got here, it may be time to see what makes you vulnerable.

What Makes You Vulnerable to Predators

Manipulators are skilled in acquiring and holding the balance of power in a relationship. They do not feel threatened or intimidated to use their skills on anyone. They feel superior to mere mortals (us). With that said, there are a few common victim traits that are similar across the board.

As a manipulator is interested in power over another, it would fit reason people who define their worth by who they are with would fit under the vulnerable heading. If you have seen the movie "Runaway Bride," Julia Roberts leaves several men at the altar, and it isn't until the end of the film that she figures out why. She never took the time to find out what she likes or who she is. If her fiancé liked boiled eggs, then our bride liked boiled eggs. If they hated ham, she hated ham. So, when her former jilted grooms got together and talked, it was like each one of them was talking about a different girl because she was simply a reflection of who they are. Once she got to know herself and what she truly liked, she was able to love. It is true; you can't love someone else if you don't love yourself first.

Another quality that hits high on the vulnerability scale is those that avoid conflict. Conflict avoiders have a hard time saying 'No' or don't have the necessary tools required to stand their ground against a person they are emotionally committed. This instance is different than our Julia Roberts bride. This person knows who they are; they just rather not fight about it. We have all been in a situation where we should have said no, and in not doing so, we overloaded ourselves with work or with too many errands as we took on more responsibility than we should have. A manipulator will zone in on this quality.

Manipulators want to tear you down. If they find someone that already has low self-esteem, they would consider that a vulnerability. Having self-confidence in who you are and your worth plays a critical role in everything that you do. Find your superpower and capitalize on the thing that you are good at to boost your confidence.

Suppose you trust people in general. Always believing that there is good in everyone because you are a quality person and operate with integrity, so why wouldn't everyone. This overview acts as a vulnerability trait. Manipulators will perform under that assumption and fly below the radar, chipping away at you until you wake up, not trusting anyone but them.

You are empathetic. You feel strongly for others and suffer with them when they endure pain or circumstance. You try to fix things. To a manipulator, this means you will never give up. You have staying power. They will twist the empathy to them and their needs, and you, being the sweet, empathetic person you are for the human condition, you will oblige.

Manipulators will try their skill on anyone, but these traits do make you more susceptible than others. Are there things that you can do to protect against manipulators? Absolutely. It does require that you see things for what they are; that is the tremendously tricky part for people with these vulnerability traits.

How to Protect Yourself From Predators

If these points are hitting close to home and you are in a relationship where you are manipulated, the only permanent way to end the manipulation is to cut it off. Severing all ties and communication with the manipulator is the only successful way to stop manipulating. Find that inner strength and say 'Adios.'

Remember that manipulators turn things around with mastery skills. If you try to reason with them, they will immediately use one of the techniques of manipulation to turn it on you. A permanent disconnection is the only – I can't say that enough – the only way to terminate the manipulation. That said, we now know what manipulators want and how they operate. They attack vulnerable, sensitive spots. How do you improve on those spots, so you do not fall victim in the future?

<u>Know Who You Are</u>. Take the time to get to know yourself. Make a date with yourself every day to learn something about what you like or don't. Stick to your guns that you do like these things, or that you don't. If a person flees from your presence because they don't like something that you hold in high value, it is not your loss; it is theirs.

<u>Self-Esteem and Self-worth</u>. Self-esteem and self-worth have a lot to do with knowing who you are and being proud of that fact. Take time to identify positive things about yourself and your accomplishments. Don't be so self-critical. Self-esteem comes in taking baby steps forward to achieve self-love. Surround yourself with people who genuinely care about you and make you feel good about yourself.

<u>Empathy Check</u>. Work with things that you can control and keep your empathy in that realm until you are strong enough to take on more. This strategy is comparable to putting on your airbag in an airplane before putting on someone else's. If you don't take care of yourself first, you will eventually crash. You can care and have empathy, just do so responsibly.

<u>Don't Be Afraid of Conflict.</u> Engaging in conflict doesn't mean you have to yell until your voice is gone. Nor does it mean you have to use vulgar language or call each other names. There are rules of engagement for conflict that, if followed, push a

relationship forward with a mutual understanding. Conflict assists in setting boundaries and is healthy if done correctly. First, you want to get to the root of the problem. Cut through all of the emotions and zone in on what is creating the conflict. The rest is just dressing. Once you establish what is indeed causing the war, then resolution can begin. Always stay calm and take a break when you need to. There is nothing that says the conflict needs to resolve in one day. If the other person is getting too agitated, take a break. Sometimes the solution presents itself during break time. Think of it as negotiation and not a fight. Finally, you won't always resolve the conflict. It is okay to have different views on a topic. The key is, you respect each other's opinions even if you disagree. It doesn't mean you need to change yours. Conflict is good; it helps us grow and opens us up to new things. Don't avoid it; embrace it.

Now, if you haven't severed ties from that manipulative relationship for whatever circumstances, such as the manipulator is a parent to your children even though you are divorced, so you have to deal with them. There are some things that you can do to prevent further manipulation.

1. <u>Their problems are not your problems</u>. No matter how much they insist that 'if only you would' or 'it's your fault,' trust yourself to know that it isn't. Do not take

on their problems or extend the courtesy of empathy their way; it will only empower them.

2. <u>Selective hearing is a necessity</u>. If the predator starts to chip away at your self-esteem, don't lower yourself to their level. Using guilt to get what they want is also a common occurrence. Put on the cone of silence and tune them out if you cannot get away from them at that precise moment. Don't acknowledge their manipulative putdowns; know your truth that they do not define you.

3. <u>Set your boundaries and stay by them</u>. Say 'No' and mean it. Do not accept that they have any power over you and do not give them any power. You control the situation. Do not avoid conflict.

4. <u>Actions speak louder than words</u>. Words are useless with manipulators. Remember who they are, remember who you are, and give them no leeway or open the door to climb back into the relationship.

5. <u>If you can cut ties</u>, cut that chord and get out.

As there are common traits among victims, there are also common traits among predators. You should be familiar with what they are to see them coming.

Predator Traits

Predators repeat the same basic behaviors because it works. Unfortunately, cases go unreported, and if they were, due to the relationship, it is more of a relationship choice and not necessarily against the law. Some manipulations are incredibly insidious but still lawful. Predators have spent years mastering their skills and fly under the radar by design, not on accident, making them all the harder to identify.

1. <u>Personal Boundaries</u>. Manipulative people have no distinguishment of what someone's boundaries are as long as they get what they want to suit their needs. They are oblivious to someone else's desires or needs if it doesn't serve their purposes. Predators are much like a toddler who sees a sucker just out of reach. If you can't afford the sucker, it merely doesn't matter. If it is an alcohol-infused sucker, it doesn't matter. There is no reasoning with a toddler if something he wants is right in front of him, just as there is no reasoning with a manipulator. What the manipulator sees is their need and someone that can fulfill it. Your boundaries simply don't matter.

2. <u>Avoidance of Responsibility</u>. Responsibility does not exist for a manipulator. Everything is the fault of the prey. They understand the concept of responsibility, but it is your job to fulfill their needs, so ultimately, it

is your fault. You carry their burden and yours. You soon become so busy with being their entire world that your world is nonexistent. They often claim to be the victim in every circumstance.

3. <u>Emotions are Tools to Use</u>. When I say emotions, I mean your emotions. Manipulators are not bothered with such things as emotions for something other than their primary need at the moment. If you are empathetic and kind-hearted, they will apply guilt as leverage. Using your feelings against you is how manipulators get power over you. You will be so blind with the obligation that it is hard to see anything else outside that tunnel. Manipulators will fake sincerity and caring to get what they want.

4. <u>Bad Mouthing Behind Backs</u>. Predators have no qualm talking poorly about others behind their backs. They are only kind, welcoming, and helpful to people if it keeps up their guise or gets them what they want. They use people as quickly as they use emotions.

5. <u>Deception</u>. Predators will hide who they are and their intentions. They will come across as helpful and play on your sympathies. Your family and friends will see which one of the faces the predator wants them to see. Manipulators are chameleons. They can blend in and morph on a dime. They can be anything they need to be to get what it is they are after.

Predators have spent years bending their surroundings into what they want them to be. They know what is socially acceptable and appealing and act the part as long as it suits them and brings them closer to what they want. They often break the rules as it suits them, but others need to follow them.

Summary

In this Chapter, we covered a lot of ground about persuasion, manipulation, victims, traits, and vulnerabilities. You should be able to:

1. Successfully identify persuasion and manipulation.
2. Successfully identify the differences between them.
3. Understand vulnerability traits
4. Understand predator traits
5. Identify what tools you have at your disposal to improve your situation if you are in a manipulative relationship and tactics to avoid future manipulation.

Understanding these concepts plays a vital role in gauging the relationships that you have with people. It also enlightens you if you are participating in less than desirable behaviors of manipulation. Let's be real; a dose of manipulation occurs in every relationship, whether it be withholding affections to doting on a loved one with the intent of getting something in return. There is a difference here. This difference just proves that we all have it inside us to commit small atrocities from time to time.

The bottom line is to leave people better than you found them. A healthy exchange of ideas and thoughts, agreeing to disagree, and navigating conflict is all healthy behavior. If this is what you do daily, you are a far cry from being a manipulative person. Interactions should always take place on level ground with respect. It is a balancing act at times, that is the price of being an individual. If it is a one-sided power play all of the time, it is time to rethink that relationship.

CHAPTER 2: THE PSYCHOLOGY OF SUCCESS

The mind is a powerful thing. If you believe in something enough, it is more likely to happen. When people think positively, the world around them seems to change. Everyone knows that one person that lives a charmed life. They are usually a positive, upbeat person who believes they can do anything while simultaneously wondering why all these good things happen to them.

The film "Field of Dreams" is an excellent example of believing in something you can't explain and having the inner strength and drive to stay focused on a mission despite how others may feel, think, and chastise you. Keven Costner believed if he built a baseball field, they (baseball players from the past) would come. Why not? It worked for Moses and his Arc. Costner and Moses both had a voice driving them on, comparable to the inner voice in our heads. This voice acts as the chamber where we weigh our decisions, create dreams, and face our demons.

The term success is defined as many things and is usually related to being 'accomplished.' You can be successful in many things. Some achieve emotional success, business success, family success, etc. Success closely matches what that little voice in your head values. If you are a successful writer, you may be unsuccessful in the family space. If you are successful in your family, you may be unsuccessful in your career space. Success is measured and defined in very different ways for different people. That's not to say that you can't be successful in several things at once; in fact, that is ideal.

For example, in the movie "Jerry Maguire," there is one scene that has always stood out in my mind as the definition of success. In a scene between Tom Cruise and Cuba Gooding, Jr., Cuba is describing what he considers being successful. In the conversation, he coined the word 'Kwan.' In his mind, it meant career, community, love, family – successfully acquiring the whole package and the money. Since that movie, a vast majority of people identified with 'becoming Ambassadors of the Kwan'.

In learning to control our emotions and harness that power, and it is power - wars have started over such things; we must understand how emotions work and where they begin.

The Trilogy of Emotions

Most people believe that how they feel is the root of where their emotions come to be. This in-the-moment feeling is partially correct. The answer is a bit more complicated than that.

Physiological Theories (Body)

Physiological Theories are the easiest to recognize. If you have ever had a crush on someone, you can feel the heat go to your cheeks. Maybe your stomach has butterflies, or you feel physically nauseous. Your pulse quickens a pace or two when your crush is around. All of these are physiological emotions and a key ingredient in our trilogy of emotions.

Cognitive Theories (Mind)

Cognitive Theories are what most people would categorize themselves. This theory correlates with common sense. Say someone cuts you off on the freeway. You think about what just occurred, decide that it is wrong, and subsequently are infuriated or annoyed. This feeling is the cause and effect of your emotions. Unlike the Physiological Theory where you get all sweaty-palmed standing next to a crush, there was an event here that caused your annoyed reaction. A great deal of these emotions centers around your interpretation of the event.

Some people may see one event in two completely different ways and have other emotions concerning the same event.

Behavioral Theories (Action)

Actions are far easier to read than trying to guess what someone is feeling or thinking. These feelings take action on the outside. If you kiss your crush or wave your fist at the rude driver who cut you off, you show your emotions through behavior. This behavior is probably the most misunderstood of the trilogy, which makes sense. You don't always act how you feel. Say, for example, kissing the crush would be inappropriate in front of his/her girlfriend/boyfriend, so you refrain. Some actions are not socially acceptable. Those are the ones we usually don't act on because social behavior discourages it.

Breaking down emotions like this is oversimplifying what emotions are on a large scale. Emotions are complicated and include a wide variety of psychological phenomena. You must include personalities, moods, motivations, and several other factors to get an accurate picture of why they feel the way they do.

For instance, say that the rude driver that cut you off was on the way to the hospital and was a bit distracted by his wife in the backseat who was going into labor. Would you still shake your fist at him, or would you foster some understanding and compassion for the situation and let him cut in. Context matters, and so does a history in the relationship that you can compare to for reference. You have no relationship history built with the freeway cutoff guy, so your first reaction is that he is a jerk. Again, a considerable oversimplification; however, these theories give you a basic working model.

Primary Emotions

The interesting thing about emotions is that you can experience several of them at once. For example, you are headed to a dentist appointment because your tooth hurts. You may be feeling anxious, afraid, and relieved that it will be taken care of finally.

Emotions and moods are not the same things. Emotions tend to be short-lived bursts of strong feelings, while moods are less intense but live for a far more extended period. Moods usually require no event, and sometimes there is simply no rhyme or reason why you feel a certain way for days on end. If emotions are the sprint, moods are the marathon.

There is an ancient book dating back centuries, where a Chinese philosopher identified seven raw emotions: joy, anger, sadness, fear, love, disliking, and liking. Speed forward to the 20th century, where the list went to six, then eight, and has now settled back to today's definition, listing six **raw** emotions.

1. Happiness
2. Sadness
3. Anger
4. Fear
5. Disgust; and
6. Surprise

The list has changed little from ancient times. The theory is that humans have a core, primary emotions that have evolved due to our world evolving around us. So, the feeling of shock amplifies surprise. Emotions blend to form hybrids, such as jealousy, which amplifies anger and fear. Enraged would stem from anger. Emotions have grown to fit the world they live in. New creations such as social media helped in this evolution. It created new things that we had to identify and then feel some kind of way about them.

Evolutions in our society are why it is important to understand emotions have evolved to adapt and describe situations around us. This evolution means that culture, family, outside influences, life experiences, and so many other things have created us and influenced how we feel, think, and behave toward our emotions as a result. People navigate interactions and situations with emotional intelligence.

Emotional Intelligence

It would stand to reason that if the population utilizes intelligence to perceive information, there would be emotional intelligence to perceive emotions. Emotional intelligence is what people use to interpret, process, and react to their emotions. Some people demonstrate better control over their emotions than others.

Daniel Goleman was the first to breach the five components of Emotional Intelligence (EI). According to Goleman, they are:

1. <u>Self-Awareness</u> – The ability to be aware of your emotions and be able to relate to other's feelings. It also refers to knowing that your behavior affects others. You seek knowledge and interaction with others because you can process new information.

2. <u>Self-Regulation</u> – This refers to taking ownership of your actions. Handling conflict in positive ways and being able to diffuse volatile situations. You are aware of how your actions affect others.

3. <u>Social Skills</u> – This refers to the ability to relate to your peers on an emotional level. These skills identify with others and communicating ideas in all forms. These social skills are where leadership and influence are born.

4. <u>Empathy</u> – This is being able to read other people's emotions accurately and respond appropriately to them. There is an understanding of the balance of power in relationships both at work and at home. You can read these situations accurately and respond accordingly.

5. <u>Motivation</u> – This is personal goals. Setting goals for yourself and achieving them for you rather than attaining them for outside sources. These people take the initiative, are ambitious, and committed to improving themselves and seeking information to do so. These are our goal setters.

Knowing these components is essential. Research supports that people with high Emotional Intelligence (EI) are more likely to succeed in life. Science has proven that people with higher EIs have higher salaries. The good news is if you do not have a high EI, you can improve it, whereas IQs are locked-in, EIs do not work the same way.

The Value of a High EI

Emotional intelligence has been linked to professional success because you can behave in a way that appeals to your peers, read situations and people well, and exhibit quality social skills. EI links to a person's happiness and general well-being. Naturally, if you can connect with the world around you and navigate every relationship and situation while having complete control and confidence – you live a charmed life. Partly because you don't see a challenge as a challenge, you see it as an opportunity and partly because you are prepared to handle any difficulty that arises. This view alone gives you real power to rise to your full potential. Not sure where you are on Emotional Intelligence? You can get a free EI test and find out what you need to work on in your emotional intelligence.

Emotional intelligence is a highly-coveted commodity trait in both the personal and professional arenas. Emotional intelligence plays a more significant role than IQ because IQ gives no guaranty that you are a successful person. Emotional intelligence, however, has powerful indications that you could be. It is all about your relationships with others, how you interact, how you lead, how you have control over your emotions to act appropriately in all circumstances, and represent yourself and the company well.

Nurturing Your Emotional Intelligence

Remember how we said EI could be improved? So, how is it that you work on your Emotional Intelligence score? There are five critical areas of focus:

1. <u>Resilience</u>. It's all about how you get up. Resilience refers to the ability to stay positive in failure or adversity. Everyone fails. You must know in your heart that the effort is worth it and rise back up to learn from that failure and build again. Resilience is being able to get back up in record speed, dust yourself off, and try again. It doesn't have to be the same route. Part of resilience is avoiding obstacles that you have run into in the past and learning from your mistakes. For example, Walt Disney, you know the name, right? Walt got turned down over 300 times before being able to create his Mouse or theme park. It pays to be resilient; you just don't know when it will pay off.

2. <u>Self-Soothing</u>. We teach this to our children at a very young age. Babies who use pacifiers are probably the

first to utilize this skill. Or, a toddler with a blanket (I must admit, I've not entirely broken that trend yet). When you initially take the pacifier away when it is time for their nap, the first few days are, well, barley endured for the both of you. But, the baby learns to sleep without it. They know to stop screaming for a parent in the middle of the night. They learn to put themselves back to sleep. How? They learn to soothe themselves rather than relying on outside sources. As adults, we forget how to do that at some point. Being able to make ourselves feel worthy and sound is a crucial skill. If you want to have the strength to take on the world and any adversity or handle harsh words and evils in this world, you need to be able to rely on yourself for comfort, encouragement, and self-love. Self-soothing is the ability to *want* to be soothed by others, but not *need* to be.

3. <u>Setting Boundaries</u>. The more famous you are, the more friends and family you find you have. There will always be parasites that want to be close to you if you do well to steal your fame to suit their purpose. In the movie "Joe Dirt," David Spade, an alleged orphan, becomes famous by telling his life story on the radio. His parents show up abruptly after he is well-known to promote their home-business of selling clowns. Joe

Dirt realizes that they are using him for his fame and promptly cuts them out of his life. His parents did not fit into his emotional boundaries. Setting boundaries is a vital part of teaching others what is and what is not acceptable behavior to you. This boundary setting is self-awareness in the highest form. You know yourself, you know what you can and can't accept, and set the rules. You teach people how to treat you. Setting boundaries is a large part of that.

4. <u>Organized Life</u>. Having an organized life means that your bills are in order, your credit score doesn't make you lose sleep, your home is in order, your career is in check, your emotional circle and your circle of trust are solid – basically, you are killing it. Being organized and controlling your life and situation means less anxiety, less stress, less drama, and less worry. What it also means is you are a happier person. If this is an area, you need to work on, sit down, and plan to get where you want to be. Take it on in reasonable segments. This planning stage is probably the most formidable goal for most.

5. <u>Fear Is Your Friend</u>. Everyone is scared of something. It is okay to feel fear, but that is when courage needs to kick in. Fear leads to doubt; doubt leads to anger;

anger leads to the dark side. You have heard this before. Fear is the biggest obstacle in a positive life. Sometimes, things just need to be put in perspective of what's the worst that could happen, or even say that you never know until you try. Don't let it be fear that leads to your failure; let it be the trying that leads to your failure. Failure is not always a bad thing and leads to several lessons in life that we need to learn to have a sense of accomplishment. We didn't learn to walk by sitting on our duff. Learning failure is important because it teaches you how to get back up.

If you work on each of these areas, you will find yourself more emotionally sound, and your Emotional Intelligence will be a bit keener. Remember that Emotional Intelligence has a direct effect in the area of your life. Learning to master these skills will significantly change your perspective and how you encounter challenges in your life. It is worth the work. You now know a bit more about emotions than you did, but will these facts help you read people?

The Art of People Watching

Some people go to the mall, and people watch. There is a whole other group that goes to Walmart to people watch. Why is it so exciting? You, as a bystander, get to glimpse into other people's lives. You get a peek at how they interact or how they parent under stress. The same people watching goes on in the social media genre. However, it isn't as raw. Pictures posed and polished, still life carefully placed for your review, while real life is messy and more entertaining.

People watching is also incredibly valuable. We had just discussed Emotional Intelligence. Knowing how people react to things, understanding their emotions, and social skills can be observed in real life taking place all around you. Watching people behave on the public stage is good practice and a first step in reading them. An empath is a term that you will find in Science Fiction. Empaths are mighty beings that can sense other people's emotions and feel them as if they were their own. You can't hide anything from them or deceive them, they will know. This inability to hide emotion is where an empath's power stems from; empathizing with other people allows them to read situations accurately and act accordingly every time.

People who are gifted at reading people are incredibly successful in endeavors, including predators. Knowing how to read people means you will learn how to read social situations, behaviors, and yes, have better luck in identifying predators at an earlier stage before they can cause any damage to you or your self-esteem.

How to Read People

When looking at how people behave in a particular situation, it is imperative to keep your personal bias out of the equation and keep an open mind. Science has shown that only 7% of our words reveal what we mean. The other tales are 55% body movement, 30% voice, and tone. If you only see the comments, you are missing more than ¾ of the conversation.

Body Language

An experiment conducted at MIT Media Lab in which researchers observed people on sales phone calls. Researchers were able to accurately predict with 87% accuracy the outcome of the sales calls simply by watching the participant's body language. Watching body language isn't categorized into any one movement. It is more of the body as a whole and asking yourself, are their body movements out of the ordinary? For example, if someone is always overly happy and excited and exclaims "GOOD MORNING" to you every morning, that is normal behavior for that person. If a person is crossing their arms, you can ask yourself if it is cold in the room? The context in which the behavior is taking place is taken into consideration. The body language technique as a whole focuses on:

1. <u>Posture</u>. Posture tends to give away demeanor and personality traits. If a person is holding their head up high, they are more than likely a confident person.

2. <u>Appearance</u>. Books are often judged by their cover; there is a reason for this. If someone shows up in yoga pants and a white tank for a job interview, you would not see them as a serious applicant because they did not take the care to show up in the appropriate gear.

3. <u>Physical Movements</u>. How a person moves is an excellent indicator of how engaged they are with you. If they perch on the edge of their chair, they are excited or anxious to hear what you have to say. The placement of their arms, hands, or even biting their lips means something. If someone clips their nails in front of you, they are either disinterested or soothing themselves because they are nervous. Remember, all motions must be taken in context and together.

4. <u>Facial Expressions</u>. Watch how they respond to questions or pictures. Faces often betray what we are feeling.

Intuitions

Your intuition is a good indicator of reading people as well. Some ways that you can start getting a read are:

1. <u>Asking Direct Questions</u>. You can ask direct questions and observe how they respond when giving a straightforward answer. Your gut feeling is usually right; go with it.

2. <u>Listen</u>. When people speak, they usually give subtle indicators of their intention or their circumstances. Understanding where they are coming from adds to being able to read them. Listen to those cues.

3. <u>Goosebumps</u>. If you get goosebumps because something they are saying is hitting home for you, this is a good sign that you are on the right track to understanding this person.

Sense Emotional Energy

You can't deny that some people just make your skin crawl to be around for whatever reason. This feeling is sensing their emotional energy. The same thing occurs while reading people. Remember the Empath we discussed; there is a little empath in all of us. Some things to look for are:

1. <u>Surrounding energy</u>. Does talking to this person feel welcoming, enticing, or do they want to make you run in the opposite direction?

2. <u>Eyes are the windows to the soul</u>. Watch the eyes. Does the person seem that they are not present with you, like almost vacant? Are they hostile?

3. <u>Hugs & Handshakes</u>. If the person physically touches you, take note of strength, confidence, shyness, aggressiveness in touch. How a person reacts in this interaction may send off signals to you.

4. <u>Tones</u>. Inflection reveals a lot about how they are feeling or interpreting the situation. Listen to everything, even the manner of their laughter. Listen carefully to what these things tell you.

Observing and being alert to the environment, the interaction, and all of the above factors will make you an astute human observer. The more you can take in, the easier it is to understand the person and their intent. Taking in information is the art of reading people.

How to Succeed

We have discussed emotions, theories, Emotional Intelligence, and how to read people. The only thing left to discuss is how to use this information. The bottom line is, people are in business. What that means is that you will talk to people every day in several different exchanges, from picking up your shirt at the drycleaners to taking a call from the Vendor that didn't deliver the pens to your office. To do well, you must be able to read those interactions and capitalize on them. You must appeal to people.

Business negotiations, mediations, everything down to asking for a raise is dependent on you being able to successfully identify with these people use mastery social skills to maneuver your position. Opportunity is not by chance; it is through action. Having these skills is known as Social Competence.

Retrain how you think and practice the following to get ahead:

1. <u>Get Personal</u>. Usually, in business, you have co-workers. Get to know them. Ask them about their work experiences, what skills they have, talk about where they went to school. All of this can fall into the category of small talk. As they let you know specific goals or skills that they have, keep this in your Rolodex. Timing is everything as we learned from Kairos. When there is a time to promote this person's particular skills in a job, do so. The insight that they give you in their experience can create a positive work environment and lift everyone to their potential.

2. <u>Attention is the Key to Good Relationships</u>. When you are talking to people, make sure that your attention is intimately on them. Silence your phone without glancing at it every two seconds. Let them know that

they are important and have your undivided attention. Ask them questions, continue to interact with them as if they are the only person in the room.

3. <u>Informal Communication</u>. Keep communications casual with your co-workers, when appropriate. This relaxed nature is to be approachable, connected, caring, and personable. Developing solid relationships is crucial in business. When they report concerns, be empathetic and understanding. Show you are personally invested in their goals.

4. <u>There is No "I" in Team</u>. Letting people know that you are there as a team member and not an individual is of profound importance. People need to feel they are working with you, that you have a common goal and a common interest. Collectively as a group, you will be able to accomplish more than you would alone and positively. A true leader doesn't need to exclaim that they are the leader. They instead lead by example in a show of positivity and camaraderie. If you practice 1 through 3 above, people are already beginning to look to you for courses of action. Let it flow.

5. <u>Recognition for a Job Well-Done</u>. Recognize those in your team for doing good work, and often. Working in

a group requires encouragement as sometimes personal differences will need to be put aside to complete the end objective. Giving plenty of praise when a job is going well and to individuals that performed exceptionally recognizes their efforts, and they are encouraged to put forth more of an effort. Who doesn't love praise?

6. <u>Motivation</u>. When you speak to people, keep your ears open for what motivates them. If you are talking to a co-worker and find they are fascinated with different kinds of cupcakes, bring cupcakes after a big project. Not all hints will be as cut and dry as that, but you get the point. Finding what moves people is the key to creating a productive work environment.

These examples to improve your business relationships translate into personal relationships as well, or academics, or any kind of relationship you are looking to build. Practicing your emotional intelligence by utilizing these tools in your daily life is a best practice. Consider that these tools cross-pollinate into every budding relationship encounter that you have.

Emotional intelligence, or what is fondly referred to as 'social currency,' is directly tied to your success. Emotional, professional, academic, relationship, or otherwise. The higher EI that you can develop, the more likely you will be to live a life that is less stressful, happier, and more fulfilling in-home, career, friends, and any other aspiration that you consider valuable.

Summary

In this Chapter, we covered emotional theories, primary emotions, emotional intelligence, reading people, and tools for increasing emotional intelligence that you can practice in everyday situations. You should be able to:

1. Identify emotions from moods.
2. Identify the five components of emotional intelligence.
3. Identify specific ways to read people.
4. Explain the benefits of emotional intelligence and know it's meaning
5. Identify practice tools to increase EQ
6. Identify EQ techniques to use in the workplace

This Chapter focuses on a great deal of positivity regarding emotions and how they can be used to your advantage. We also covered how to strengthen self-confidence and the importance of self-soothing. This knowledge will prove essential as we start delving into the rest of this book, which has far less positivity.

As you begin the journey into the next chapters, think about how the skills from this Chapter could assist you. Think about where you would be able to inject your skills into the situation to diffuse or improve upon it, or if it would be better to walk away.

54

CHAPTER 3: THE WORLD OF DECEPTION & MANIPULATION

We briefly touched on manipulation in Chapter 1. This Chapter designs to delve deeper into the world of dark manipulation and its cohort 'deception.' There is always a bit of deceit in every manipulation. We see manipulation every day, and we are familiar with manipulating circumstances to our advantage. Everyone manipulates in a small fashion here or there; it is part of the human condition. Parents are probably the most guilty in this endeavor. My mother had manipulated me into eating green veggies most of my life. Knowing that fact alone will help you grow and navigate situations where you feel you are abused. Remember, the intent always plays an essential role in any interaction. You should always be observant of what motivates this person to manipulate you, what do they want? Remember, manipulations are not as destructive as long as there is balance. So, when does manipulation grow into deception-based manipulation?

If manipulation twists the truth, deception breaks it. Deception is changing someone's perception of reality with lies to some gain of the deceiver. This deception is where we enter the realm of dark psychology, and it's first tools are deception and manipulation. Dark psychology refers to the skills of manipulation, deception, coercion, and dark persuasions that predators use to get what they want.

Dark Psychology Triad

To better explain the different types of deception and deceptive forms of manipulation, you should always look at the intent of the person you are engaging in. To do this, you utilize the skills that we covered in the first chapters. Body language, emotional intelligence skills, and signs for when you are being manipulated, it all comes together here. There are three parts in the dark psychology triad:

1. <u>Narcissism</u> – This is someone who feels superior to others and has no qualms about using others for their benefit. They are highly selfish and do not feel empathy for others. They often believe their actions to be quite marvelous and are the epitome of a 'drama queen,' including the full-on tantrums that can be abusive.

2. <u>Machiavellianism</u> – This refers to a person that exploits other people with little to no sense of morality. They would sell their grandmother to get what they want. There is no 'too far' for this person.

3. <u>Psychopathy</u> – Psychopaths are friendly and charming, the perfect storm of what we see as ideal attributes in character. They put on a great show for anyone who is watching and mask their true intentions. They are incredibly impulsive, selfish, and do not feel empathy or remorse for other people. Several famous serial killers sit in this realm. Not all psychopaths are serial killers; in fact, most aren't.

We touched briefly on covert manipulation in Chapter 1. Covert manipulation is when you break a person down by attacking their confidence and self-worth. Covert manipulation is one of the many tools of dark psychology triad.

Covert Manipulation

There are many ways in which covert manipulation tactics keep power with the manipulator in a relationship. You could fill a stadium with many tactics and skills out there, but these are the most common. A few of them are:

1. <u>Love Flooding</u>. The manipulator showers you with gifts, attention, compliments, and affection to the point that you are almost drowning. This love flooding creates and strengthens the bond between you.

Remember, the manipulator is after power, always power, so giving you all of this love and attention, it will be tough for you to say 'no' and you will become dependent on it, as well as feel the absence when it is gone. These are tools to bind you to them and make you dependent, compliant, and in control.

2. <u>No Love For You</u>. Now that you are enticed with the romance and gifts, it is time to take that away. If you do not behave appropriately in a manipulator's mind and abide by their rules, they will pull out or become absent altogether until you 'earn' it back. This restriction of love furthers your bond with them as you give up other things to pay special attention to them to win back their devotions.

3. <u>Guilt Is The Weapon</u>. Manipulators will play upon your emotions and use passive-aggressive behavior. They will not quite confront or argue with you, but rather leave subtle hints to get you to behave accordingly. Manipulators will use your empathy and feed it guilt and sarcasm to get you to do what they want.

4. <u>Semantic Manipulation</u>. Semantic manipulation refers to the manipulator saying words and then later saying they don't share the same definition of those words as you do. In this way, they didn't break the agreement because they simply had a different understanding of

it. We all remember Clinton's definition of 'sexual relations' was not the same as the American public's definition of 'sexual relations,' so, in his mind, he did not commit what he was accused of because the descriptions didn't match up.

5. <u>Social Embarrassment/Mind Games</u>. Social embarrassment refers to being in public with the manipulator, and they demonstrate their superiority through domination tactics with you to make you look simple or embarrass you. This mind game is part of taking down your self-esteem.

6. <u>Gaslighting</u>. Gaslighting is when you know that something occurred, and they immediately say 'it is all in your mind,' or 'that never happened' to make you doubt what you have seen or heard. Nothing rocks self-doubt like gaslighting. It makes you depend on the manipulator to interpret what you see and hear. This behavior is especially insidious and cruel.

The dark triad personality traits are not the only people that use covert manipulation. It is around us every day. We see it in politicians, lawyers, teachers, you name it. What I am getting at here is there is no real way to stop dark manipulation; the practice of these things isn't illegal. Knowing about the tactics is only half the battle. The key is not to allow yourself to be manipulated and have the tools to fight back. Now, where does deception fit?

Deception

Deception is hidden behind a mask. Although there are bits and pieces sprinkled in deceptive manipulations like covert manipulation, there are levels of deception. They are harder to spot, and you must look at the intent as you receive the information. Deception is getting someone to accept what is not their accurate belief. Deception steals view from the truth and has the victim believing in a false reality that the manipulator created.

Levels of Deception

1. <u>Advanced</u>. (Run). Advanced deception is used by psychopaths, serial killers, sociopaths, criminal mindset types. They are skilled deceivers with years and years of practice and a persona that is quite likable because they can be whatever they need to be to get what they want. They are actual social chameleons. They have no problem using you for whatever purpose they need and have no empathy for how you feel about it. This group contains smooth operators that can navigate your emotions

as if they live in your head. They are mastery level ninjas at the abuse techniques. If you feel that someone is in your head, they usually are.

2. <u>Above Average</u>. (Run). This group contains narcissists, personality disorders, and love them and leave them types (without the love). They have an established record of using covert manipulation to get what they want; however, you will not know about it because these types are very good at hiding who they are. Their reality is a bit off, and they want to pull you in with them to see things the way that they do. They are also fans of abusive techniques and have little to no empathy for how you feel about things.

3. <u>Slightly Above Average</u>. (Proceed with caution). These are usually people who have personality traits for deception. They typically don't know that they are behaving deceptively. They don't seem to connect with why their actions would be deceptive. When these deceivers are wrong, they will argue strictly from emotion and not logic, because they understand they are wrong, but know that if these types press, these people can get their way by merely exhausting the person they are talking with. Slight above-average deceivers are incredibly persistent.

4. <u>Average</u>. (The usual suspects). This group includes the average, everyday Joe. For example, teenage rebels trying to create autonomy and get away with as much as possible. Defiant people fall into this category. They like identifying as rebels, so their deception is far more apparent. They are not nearly as skilled as the advanced or above average deceivers and usually spotted reasonably quickly if you are looking.

In knowing these levels of deception, you will learn more about what you are dealing with. The University of Florida created a Dirty Dozen rating scale that is a 12-point methodology test that measures the personality traits of the dark psychology triad. The higher the score, the more likely the person is to have those personality traits.

Oliver James, a psychologist, had indicated that "...having Dark Triad tendencies can give someone a nefarious advantage in the workplace, in terms of career and progression." This behavior can be comparable to the positive resources of emotional intelligence – the dark triad is the negative side to emotional intelligence. As you attempt to increase your emotional intelligence, predators will improve their skills and overpower it.

We have established how emotional intelligence can play a significant role in progressing yourself and others in the workplace and your overall quality of life. The Dark Triad operates in direct conflict to that, setting out to unravel everything accomplished through positive goals and twisting it to the anti-workplace with greed, bullying, and self-indulgence.

Another movie example is necessary. Michael Douglas in "Wall Street" is the epitome of a selfish wolf chanting 'Greed is Good' in his portrayal of the wolf business-man. He doesn't care who he takes down, and any relationship with him is toxic. The movie is fantastic and a must-see, but the character he plays is lethal to any business or association.

If you have the unfortunate experience of working with someone like this in the workplace, remember the skills given in Chapter 2 and practice them religiously. Emotional intelligence skills. Remember, these types of people hide who they are and can operate with extreme efficiency in damaging any working relationships within the workplace and the business itself. If you see this type of behavior, it should be dealt with quickly before the wolf's teeth are allowed to sink in.

Dark Triad Personality Traits

The Dirty Dozen test magnifies the inherent personality traits of people in the dark triad. People associated with the dark triad usually have the following personality traits.

Narcissistic Traits

Narcissists are domineering with a deep sense of entitlement. Their primary focus is on their self-interest and personal gain. They tend to exaggerate their skillset and believe they have accomplished much more than what they have. There is no real long-term goals or planning as they are impulsive and focus only on immediate gratification at the moment. They want you to stumble over yourself, telling them how wonderful they are, so it would make sense that they are not fans of constructive criticism in any form. They have several of the same characteristics as a spoiled child. Their reputation and how others see them is of paramount importance, so they will go to great lengths to protect that image, including violence. Their deep sense of entitlement allows them to believe this behavior is acceptable.

Machiavellianism Traits

Machiavellianism contributes cunning and intensely dark manipulations to the triad. They are amoral and do not feel bound by the same code of ethics and morals as a society, so they have no problem changing their views and will take whatever action they need to get what they want. With no sense of ethics or morals, they are a dangerous bit of business. Oddly, they do not like confrontation, so they will use manipulation to bend the will of others rather than take on a direct argument, which adds to their knack of not taking the blame for anything and instead, shift it to someone else. On the flip side of that, they don't hesitate to take credit for other's achievements. Machiavels have an inherent distrust of others. They calculate every move they make and keep their mask down tight, never showing who they are. Unlike the Narcissists, they are not like children; they cannot tolerate childlike behaviors and believe it is a lack of intelligence. Their weakness is that they do have a fear of failure; they feel a strong need to be perfect in every situation. When you combine their need for perfection with the knowledge that they will do anything to be perfect, it makes for a dangerous combination.

Psychopathy Traits

When we think psychopaths, serial killers probably pop right to the forefront of your mind. Not all psychopaths fit that mold, but many of us have a little bit of psychopathic tendency. Some facts that may startle you:

- 1% of the population in the US are psychopaths (That's 3 million folks)

- 21% of CEOs have clinically significant psychotic tendencies. (That's 1 in 5)

If those numbers don't concern you, they should. These percentages mean that the likelihood of you working with someone or being in a relationship with someone that has psychopathic traits is HIGH. Psychopaths fail to acknowledge any type of remorse or empathy and use dark manipulations consistently to their advantage. They will lie about anything and everything avoiding any sense of personal responsibility and blame shift. What makes them even more dangerous is that they are unpredictable, coupled with little to no regard for the social norms that bind society. Instead, they feel that they can control others through their charm and manipulative behaviors and are inherently entitled to do that. This behavior is reinforced because they are good at it. Because of their lack of a connection with people, they are overtly bold and impulsive.

All of the dark triad personalities have a lack of empathy for anyone and participate in self-serving behavior. The dark tried is using people as a means to an end. All three characters use deceptive and manipulative practices to acquire what they want. Most importantly, all three are not afraid to use abusive tactics. If you think you are in a relationship with someone that may is considered to be in the dark triad, there are ways to deal with it but do consider getting outside help.

How to Cope With the Dark Triad

Each type in the dark triad has specific kinds of behavior. If you find yourself in a work environment or relationship with a member of the dark triad, there are some things that you can do to protect yourself.

Coping With Narcissists

Narcissists are incredibly bright and extremely astute at harvesting people's emotions and repurposing them for their own needs and purposes. Narcissists have unshakeable delusions of grandeur. They are demi-gods on the face of the earth. They believe that all of the ways they use people are acceptable because they are unique. This view plays out in their interactions with people.

The massive difference here is that they are easier to manage than Psychopaths or Machiavellianism. The personality traits of a Narcissist are much like a spoiled child that cannot see outside of their own needs. You would set the same boundaries that you do with a child. If you want to get on their good side, or you are at work and need to get a project done, these are things that will help you in that endeavor:

<u>Flatter them</u>. Remember that Narcissists are all about themselves; giving them praise and recognition is the most direct way to get their attention. Tell them how dashing they are, how their hair shines, or how intelligent they are. Lavish them with compliments. It will put their guard down.

<u>Immediate reward</u>. If you want these people to do something, setting up an immediate gratification reward is extremely helpful. Remember, they do not think long-term; everything is at the moment.

<u>Recognition</u>. Narcissists are like children, and when you put a child in the spotlight, they beam with pride. During the job, tell them how extremely well they are doing and give praise and plenty.

DO NOT tell them they are wrong or challenge their authority (even if it is in their mind) in public. Remember that reputation is the one thing that narcissists hold near and dear to their heart, so use that as a point of motivation.

Making them look good = YES
Making them look bad = NO

Once you recognize and accept what Narcissist motives are, you will successfully navigate the relationship into something that you can work with if you are forced to do so. Honestly, this relationship is to be avoided as there is no give and take; there is only take.

Coping With Machiavellianism

Dealing with Machiavellianism requires the ability to self-soothe and have a strong sense of who you are with the strength of conviction in your beliefs. Emotional intelligence skills are of paramount importance in this situation. The critical thing to remember here is don't make known any emotion you feel; hold them close. The primary tool of Machiavellianism is manipulation, so the second they get something on you, they will zone in on it and use it against you in the most amoral of ways. Remember, there are no ethics or morals that they adhere to, so arguing is pointless. The best way to accomplish anything with Machiavellianism is:

1. <u>Public Agreement</u>. Unlike the Narcissist, this is one that you will want to get a verbal agreement from in a public setting. They do not like confrontation and don't want to be in the spotlight so that they may agree. If it is in a public situation, they are more likely to do

what you need them to do to keep flying below the radar.

2. <u>Shift Your Chess Pieces</u>. Always be thinking ahead. Remember that Machiavels move people as chess pieces, including who you may believe are on your side, they will go to work on them. Know who you are working with, who you can trust, who is a threat, and who is unsure. Your inner Machiavel will need to come out to navigate this situation and keep the ball in your court.

3. <u>Make Them Look Good</u>. Machiavels are more pliable when making them look good in situations and won't be guarded if they think you are already on board with their plan. Look for insights on their motivations. If you can find that, it will give you a bit more leverage in motivating them to go the direction you want to go.

Coping With Psychopaths

Psychopaths are probably the hardest to deal with out of the three in the dark triad because they are incredibly successful at what they do. They have qualities that put them in an authoritative position and are intelligent enough to seize an opportunity when they see it. They are sophisticated and charming and operate with confidence in the fact that they can easily control others.

Remember that as they don't feel empathy and are not held by social norms, the reasoning is ineffective. Psychopaths are not easily intimidated. They are the intimidators and have successfully manipulated and outright lied to be in the position that they are. They will bend every social norm to stay there, which is farther than most will go. A one-on-one conversation is ill-advised when dealing with one.

When dealing with a psychopath, you must keep in mind that whatever you say can be turned around and lied about easily. The last thing you want with a psychopath is their word against yours. In that same regard, don't believe anything that they say.

<u>Watch Your Back</u>. Psychopaths lie. They will do underhanded things to move themselves up in an organization, including backstabbing you or taking credit for your work. They will undermine your authority to raise theirs. They do this with alarming skill.

<u>Moving On</u>. Psychopaths generally don't stay in one place for too long. Because they do lie, karma does come around eventually. They will move on when the opportune moment

to do so is at hand, just before everything falls to pieces and you are left to clean it up. The best thing to do is to avoid a psychopath. If you can't, stay on defense until they destroy every opportunity they have and jump ship.

It is not an ideal game plan to watch something that you have helped build be systematically taken apart by a psychopath, but the alternative is allowing them to take you down as well. The better solution is to have the strength and courage to put the pieces back together after they have left. Psychopaths are the epitome of a parasite that lives in its host until the host can no longer support its needs, and it finds a new host to suck the life out.

How to Heal After These Abusive Relationships

We have discussed what you should do if you see the power struggle and manipulation in a relationship coming, but what about it you didn't see it coming? If you have just been the victim of an abusive relationship of any one of these three personality types, you have a road of healing in front of you. You may be feeling uses, empty, unsure of who you are, and overwhelmed with where you should begin. Some things that you can do to help you through it are:

Recognize What Happened

You must start recognizing what happened in the relationship. Realizing why you felt and not what you felt is the place to start. Understanding why you had the feelings you did allows you to see certain red flags in the relationship and reflect on them. If you can pinpoint the 'whys,' you can manage your emotions more effectively and recognize that feeling in any future relationships as a warning sign. Recognition will allow you to develop distancing techniques and stepping away from the connection to gain the perspective of someone looking into the relationship.

It is helpful to write the experience down to analyze it more effectively. Converting the relationship to the page allows you to review the conditions you were living in and provides more insight into things that you may not have seen happening at the time.

Recognize That It's Not Everyone

When you read through your journal, pick specific incidents to apply it to all men or all women. Such as, "All men are controlling" or "All women are controlling," then remind yourself that it is not valid. Separate the behavior from 'all' to 'one.' One person treated you poorly. One person was controlling. You don't want to blame an entire gender for what one person did. Healing requires you to see things as they were so you can appropriately process them.

Love Thyself

You have been broken. It is time to get to know yourself so you can develop a love for yourself. Start working on your emotional intelligence skills as well as be compassionate towards yourself.

1. <u>Don't judge yourself harshly</u>. Forgive yourself, be kind. You felt that you were with another person because they lied to you. They hid their identity. You are not a fool; you encountered a person that was incredibly good at deceit and manipulation.

2. <u>It could happen to anyone</u>. Narcissists exert their skills on the entire population that they encounter. Anyone could have been in your shoes just as quickly. Unfortunately, you won't be their last victim. It's all about the getting up, don't blame yourself, but do learn from it.

3. <u>Know your feelings</u>. Explore the pain of your emotions. Permit yourself to go through the wide range of emotions that you are experiencing and to identify why you are feeling them. Don't relive your emotions daily, but do be able to identify your feelings correctly.

4. <u>Tell yourself you are loved and valued.</u> Be sure to shower yourself with praise while you lick your wounds. You are compassionate; you are worthy, you have people that love you, you are strong, hold all of your virtues up to the light and take them within yourself, believing every word of it. Transform the thinking from 'victim' to 'survivor.'

Focus On Your Interests

It is time to explore what your hobbies are. Take an interest in your health and well-being. Try something new and figure out what you like to do. Spend time with family and friends that you feel good being around. Stay busy, immersing yourself into new positive experiences. Staying active will build up your confidence and get you in the right headspace while working on your emotional intelligence skills.

Seek Professional Help

You need someone to talk to that can help make sense of your emotions and build your self-confidence and self-worth back up. You have the inner strength; you must have someone guide you through the rocky terrain. These types of relationships are not easy to get over because they are incredibly invasive, intense, and have changed your perception of what you thought you knew. Having a guide is essential to self-discovery.

The Light Triad

Ironically, a light triad mirrors the dark, but with positivity. It makes sense, as the world needs balance. The items in the light triad aren't the opposite of the dark triad items; there is more to it. Scientists concluded three distinct factors:

1. <u>Kantianism</u> – this is about treating people as people and not as a means to an end.
2. <u>Humanism</u> – this is about valuing the worth in each individual
3. <u>Faith in humanity</u> – this is about believing that humans are fundamentally good.

People that scored high on the Light Triad tend to:

1. Be able to have tolerance with other people's perspectives
2. Be secure in who they are and their relationships
3. Do not need to have power over others in any way
4. Demonstrate humility and have an agreeable nature about them
5. Satisfied with their life and are curious about things

The Light Triad is not theoretically connected to the dark triad and has its own separate, distinct personality traits. The research is promising, and there is much to be discovered as we stroll down this new branch in the psychological tree.

The Dark Triad focuses on negative aspects and destructive behavior that has hurt a lot of people and destroyed businesses and relationships. Although these people may be successful in life, it is not a good thing. So, how are we to be successful in life without being less than a desirable person. The Light Triad may be able to demonstrate precisely how to do that by showing the link of the light triad with positive characteristics, such as:

"Quiet Ego," which focuses on perspective-taking, inclusive identity, detached awareness, and growth-mindedness.

Research evidence supported that all of us have a little good and a little bad. Remember those levels of deception; everything is intent and context. There are several studies still being conducted regarding the Light Triad and its implications. You can even be a part of it by taking the test to see if you are a member of the Light or Dark Triad.

Summary

In this Chapter, we covered the Dark Triad and the personalities that lie within. These are people that are in your everyday lives more than you may have realized. You should now know how to identify these critical Dark Triad personality traits and how to navigate them. You should also have a better understanding of the tools they use to achieve their goals and what you can do to motivate them to work for you towards a common goal in the workplace or a relationship.

Emotional intelligence skills play a crucial role in handling the three personality types of the Dark Triad. At this point, you should understand how to utilize your skills to assist you with combating the personality types of the Dark Triad. You must be aware of when you are being manipulated to prevent it from occurring.

The Dark Triad is a particularly dangerous combination because of the lack of empathy and failure to adhere to social norms and ethical rules of engagement. You must always be aware of the fact that their limits know no bounds, and they have no qualms about taking whatever 'weakness' or emotion that you give them and twisting it.

If you can recognize these dark qualities, you can set proper boundaries and protect yourself against such mechanisms. Remaining vigilant to these personality types and traits and why they behave the way they do, is the best way to avoid falling victim to them.

The Light Triad shows promise in further exploring the positive side of the human condition. In contrast to the Dark Triad, it focuses on the good in humanity and how having these traits can work for you complimentary to your emotional intelligence skills. Research is in its beginning stages. There is the possibility that having too many characteristics of the Light Triad can work against you by being susceptible to the Dark Triad skillset of manipulation. This imbalance is why emotional intelligence may play a key role in balancing out too much of a good thing.

Healing after someone has taken advantage of you takes far longer than avoiding the occurrence in the first place. This Chapter provided the tools to identify, navigate, and protect yourself from situations in your everyday life.

CHAPTER 4: THE POWER OF HYPNOSIS

Hypnosis is an area that is shrouded in mystery and intrigue since ancient times. Hypnosis has been a part of every single culture throughout existence. The Egyptians called it 'temple sleep.' Egyptians would have the subject ingest various herbs and other ingredients. The person hypnotized would be led to a dark chamber and sleep, awaiting their dreams to provide insight into whatever was ailing them, which would reveal the cure.

This practice spread to the Greeks, who called them 'sleep temples.' The Greeks would feed the subject various herbs and exercise everything the Egyptians did, except they would fill the chamber with snakes, the god's symbol. Ancient peoples used hypnosis as a connection to the divine and in healing. Hypnosis amplifies an Oracle's ability to speak of fortune and the future. The Oracle and the subject would drink herbal mixtures together and sit in a chamber occupied by candles and bright paintings on the wall. This lively ambiance intensified suggestibility in the mind of the subject, making them more susceptible to the experience and suggestion of the Oracle.

In the movie "300", Pythia was an Oracle-based off the Oracle of Delphi. The Oracle of Delphi was known as one of the most potent Oracles. Spartans would not wage war unless the Oracle Pythia projected a positive outcome. If she didn't, they wouldn't fight. Spoiler alert, Leonidis did not listen and therefore sealed his fate.

The use of hypnosis is continuing its tradition throughout the ages. Hypnosis was even used in the Civil War by doctors on soldiers before amputation. Besides its healing powers, it was discovered that hypnosis could also control pain and discomfort.

The History of Hypnosis in Psychology

Although all cultures use Hypnotism throughout time, it wasn't until the 1700s that hypnosis started gaining ground in Psychology as a field of study. However, it wasn't called hypnosis at the time and wouldn't be until the 1800s. In the 1700s, it was referred to as Mesmerism. To understand where we are going, we need to know where we have been and how far Hypnotism has come and evolved. Each pioneer in the field brought a little something and perfected theories and methods. This perfection of the craft is a highlighted brief history, not by any means, is it a complete list. But, it will provide some insight as to how hypnosis evolved over several hundreds of years to the results we have today.

The 1800s – Mesmer created theories on healing by magnetism. These theories dated back to Paracelsus. Paracelsus created laudanum in the 1400s and was the first to pioneer in making chemicals into functional medicines. Mesmer believed in 'animal magnetism.' He did not hypnotize anyone; instead, he healed by channeling magnetism into his patients.

Mesmer acquired some followers, such as Marquis de Puysegur, who induced a state called 'artificial somnambulism' in his patients. He believed this sleep-like state of being a supernatural process.

Braid came onto the scene and was a critic of Mesmerism. He thought the techniques to be pseudoscientific supernatural theory. So, he modified the techniques and coined the term 'hypnotism' and 'hypnotic therapeutics' describing his approach. He used focused attention and suggestion. Braid is considered the pioneer of Hypnotism as opposed to its predecessor, Mesmerism.

The 1900s – Pavlov, the Nobel Prize physiologist, conducted experiments based on the physiological model of Hypnotism.

His studies in Hypnotherapy were the basis of Soviet psychotherapy for decades.

Freud had a hand in popularizing the concept of hypnotic regression therapy but left the theory shortly after for the psychoanalytic method.

Coue created the theory of Conscious Autosuggestion, which abandoned a sleep-state. His tours promoted this self-help method.

Janet, a French psychiatrist, is held as one of the leading pioneers in psychotherapy. He coined the term 'subconscious' and the concept of psychological dissociation. His psychotherapy emphasized Hypnotism, and his views influenced several psychotherapists.

The 1930s – Hull, President of the American Psychological Association, is a significant person in behavioral psychology. His research team completed laboratory research on Hypnotism and published *Hypnosis & Suggestibility*. This book is regarded as the first significant scientific document on hypnosis and inspired several researchers to investigate hypnosis.

<u>The 1960s</u> – Erickson is considered one of the most influential hypnotists of the 20th century. He developed the use of 'indirect' suggestions in Hypnotherapy.

Hilgard developed the Stanford Hypnotic Susceptibility Scales with Weitzenhoffer. He also created the 'neo-dissociation' theory of hypnosis and was known as an authority on hypnotic pain control.

Sarbin was a fan of the nonstate theory of hypnosis. This theory means without putting your subject in a heightened state. His research inspired the 'cognitive-behavioral' approaches to hypnosis.

<u>The 1980s</u> – Orne, a Professor of Psychiatry and Psychology at the University of Pennsylvania, was central to the research on social 'demand characteristics' and how hypnosis drew upon both a state and nonstate perspective of hypnosis. He was a pioneer in false memory and how the use of hypnosis could distort recalling events.

Barber developed a nonstate approach called the 'cognitive-behavioral' theory of hypnosis. In producing vast amounts of evidence for this theory, he indicated no 'special state' but was the psychological process as cognition and behavior such as imagination, motivation, and expectation.

Hypnotism was molded through various efforts by researchers in several different fields. Psychology and how the mind works taps into several separate areas, so it is only natural that people want to be a part of its study to see how it may benefit their field. Now that we have uncovered Hypnotism's roots, we can adequately define it.

What Is Hypnotism

Hypnosis is defined as 'a trance-like state in which you have a heightened focus and concentration' according to the Mayo Clinic. In this trance, you are open to suggestion, calm, and relaxed. In this heightened state of awareness, you are still in control of everything going on around you, but you are calm enough not to be distracted by the obvious. It allows your mind not to be overwhelmed with stimulation and focus on gaining insight.

Have you ever been driving in your car and arrive at your destination, startled because you don't remember how you got there? It is a bit disorienting, and you could say you were in a trance-like state. No? How about that time when you were half asleep, though you didn't know it, and someone pounds on your door, snapping you back to alert right quick. Both places are a state of hypnosis. So, our minds certainly can enter a trance-like state where we are calm and relaxed, even without a therapist in the room, although having one is highly recommended if you will give it a go.

In hypnosis, you do not lose control of your bodily functions. It is not mind control—hypnosis centers around suggestions. When you are relaxed and receptive, you are far more ready to take a few suggestions to alter or control some undesirable behaviors.

As we have seen, there are several theories and schools of thought that have developed over the years leading us to several different branches down the same tree. Hypnosis is used to control undesired behaviors or help you cope with pain. There are three primary methods to administer hypnosis:

Guided Hypnosis

This type of hypnosis is comparable to the Pied Piper. He is the chap that played his flute and guided the rats out of London. In guided hypnosis, you use tools such as music or a recorded voice, or the ticking of a clock to induce you into a hypnotic state. The instrument being the Pied Piper's flute guiding you to your destination. In today's time, there are mobile apps that can administer this type of hypnosis.

Hypnotherapy

This type of hypnosis is utilized in psychotherapy. A licensed physician or psychologist will use Hypnotherapy to treat depression, anxiety, post-traumatic stress disorder, and other behavioral disorders.

Self-Hypnosis

Self-hypnosis is the process of putting yourself in a hypnotic state without the use of tools, just the use of your mind. It is used as a self-soothing tool to control pain and stress. This self-hypnosis would be a useful tool to couple with emotional skills of self-soothing and controlling your emotions.

Our Subconscious Mind

It is confusing when talking about separating the conscious mind from the subconscious mind. Sigmund Freud created the psychoanalytic theory of personality. He defined the unconscious mind as one's thoughts, feelings, urges, and memories outside the range of conscious awareness.

This theory means that in the outside, unconscious range, we have pain, anxiety, and conflict. These are not pleasant feelings, nor do we like discussing them. Freud believed that these unconscious feelings influence your behaviors, even though you are not aware of it.

It may be easier to understand this concept if you think of an island. Everything on the island's surface, you can see and are aware it exists. It is easy to understand. That would be your conscious mind. You only see the surface of the island. However, under the water is a mass amount of land that you don't see. That is the subconscious. You know it is there, but most of the time, you walk around unaware of it. If the ocean drained and you could see the entire island, you would be on an immense mountain.

So, in theory, it is the unconscious thoughts that cause unpleasant problems. Anger, compulsive behaviors, poor social interactions, and relationship problems can stem from unrest in the unconscious self. If we repress these unpleasant emotions, they are held in our subconscious. Repression also includes urges. Freud believed that life and death instincts lived in the unconscious as well. Life instincts refer to procreation and survival. Death instincts refer to trauma and danger. The term Freudian slip refers to accidentally saying out loud what is in our subconscious thoughts.

People do not live out loud with what is in their subconscious. They much prefer to keep that secret and be unaware that it exists. In bringing these thoughts to light, the theory goes that you will find the source of the unrest and address it. If addressed, Freud believed it would relieve psychological distress. Hypnotism and Hypnotherapy allow you to be in a heightened sense of awareness so that you can see beneath the island's surface. There are a few different ways in which to bring the subconscious out to awareness.

Free Association

Free Association is when a patient is encouraged to discuss anything that comes to mind during a session. The goal is to have the patient feel comfortable enough to share anything with any preconceived judgment or notions wiped away. Freud took the hypnosis method and started replacing the model to avoid suggestions. I know this is a little distant from hypnosis relying entirely on suggestion; however, Hypnotism is at the root. Also, free association is a proven way to relax a patient that is resistant at first.

The back and forth interaction that takes place in a welcoming, safe environment is the ideal atmosphere to reach into the subconscious. Hypnotherapy takes such an approach, and we will be covering that later. The theory is that when we talk, we send a message using by using specific words. When in a relaxed state and speaking freely, 'slips' will come out that offer insight into what lies in our subconscious. The therapist encourages the patient by letting go of their self-control and defensive feelings that hide the unconscious feelings.

The critical thing in the free association is allowing the patient to get so immersed in the discussion that they are carried away with their thoughts. When this occurs, valuable insight is given into their unconscious, so issues that are haunting the patient can be addressed.

Dream Interpretation

Another way to reach the subconscious is through dream interpretation. Dream interpretation is noting down what your dreams are and then analyzing them to find the meaning. Freud believed that the unconscious mind would hide in dreams so you would be able to extract them that way. Hidden is the keyword here. Things in dreams would be manifestations of your unconscious, so they would need to be translated to items that are occurring in your conscious mind.

For example, if a dove kept reappearing to you while you had dinner with your spouse in your dream, it may be telling you to find peace in an argument. Freud believed that people could not keep their subconscious kept under lock and key when they sleep. So, in theory, the subconscious would play a vivid role in your dreams. If dreams were analyzed correctly, the root of the unrest might be found to treat it.

Continuous Flash Suppression

Continuous flash suppression is when images are displayed without people paying attention because they are distracted by a different visual display. The idea is that the picture doesn't resonate with your conscious mind; however, it does settle into your subconscious mind. Things that we see, or better yet, don't see with our conscious mind, can impact our behavior nonetheless.

People retain the image that they did not see while distracted. Research has shown that when an image is paired with a negative unconscious image, people will report more feelings of negativity when rating the impression that they saw with their conscious. This 'invisible picture' plays a role in subliminal messaging and suggestion. You may not be consciously aware of why you are doing something, but it could relate to seeing something on an unconscious level.

Subliminal messaging is thought to be a powerful force. Research has shown that subliminal messages do have some effect, especially when it is related to desire. Advertisers use subliminal messaging, but is it more than mere suggestion?

Hypnotic Suggestion vs. Subliminal Messaging

Hypnotic suggestion and subliminal messaging both make their way into our subconscious mind. They are not the same thing. Hypnosis is comparable to a participator sport. The patient has to want to be hypnotized and believes that it can work. They retain full use of their mind. There is a heightened sense of conscious awareness. You are aware of your surroundings, and all that is being said. When you are in that hypnotic state, your subconscious is more open to receiving information. Subliminal messaging is a different animal.

Researchers agree that subliminal messages do work, but not on a large scale. Princeton University conducted a study in which the word 'thirsty' was added to 12 frames of "The Simpsons" with 12 frames of Coca-Cola. Audience members did report that they were thirstier after the show.

Researchers in the Netherlands successfully got their subjects to choose Lipton iced tea as the drink of choice. British researchers conducted a study playing French and German music in a wine section of a supermarket. On the days' French music was played, 77% of the customers purchased French wine. As you would suspect, on the German music days, most patrons bought German wine.

You would think that overall, the results were positive, showing that subliminal messaging works. However, it is still seen as having limited effectiveness. The reason being is it isn't clear how long the effect lasts. Sure, after you finish an episode of the Simpsons, you want a Coca-Cola, but what about two hours after, do you still want it or has the feeling passed?

Researchers indicate that subliminal messaging will make something that we were already predisposed to doing more enticing to do. So, if we dislike Coca-Cola, it is not likely that we would be reaching for one anytime soon. Subliminal messages cannot change our minds. It is unknown if subliminal messaging works well or not in advertising.

Subliminal messaging is one of those things that looks good on paper with all of the positive results but is limited in its use because longevity is unknown. Subliminal messaging could be perfected at some point in the future to be used more frequently with more power, but at present, it amplifies something you were going to do anyway.

Hypnosis offers the staying power that subliminal messaging doesn't quite have mastered yet. Subliminal messaging is something that we are not aware of consciously, while hypnosis ensures we are aware of everything. Those are the two most considerable differences between the two.

Something tells me that if advertisers are ever able to master the skills of subliminal messaging, a great deal of money will be poured into it if it develops any real kind of staying power.

Hypnosis has the added challenge of needing someone to by hypnotizeable. Subliminal messages do not share this challenge. Subliminal messaging does not have a 'type.' It appears to work on all populations. Hypnosis needs motivation. This difference could be that subliminal speaks directly to our subconscious mind. Our conscious awareness well guards the gateway to the subconscious mind in hypnosis. There is no barrier like that with subliminal messaging, which is why it may prove ideal in the advertising realm.

Who Can Be Hypnotized

It is thought that 25% of the population cannot be hypnotized because they are skeptical and do not see the benefits of Hypnotism and are unwilling participants. This percentage leaves an overwhelming 75% of the population that can be. Some of the community has traits that lead them to be more susceptible to being hypnotized. These traits are called their 'hypnotizability.' To be successfully put into hypnosis, you must be a willing participant, and you must possess at least a minimal degree of hypnotizability.

Hypnotizability

Psychologists have been studying what traits make someone more susceptible to Hypnotism over other people without much success. There are, however, a few traits that have been higher correlated to hypnotizability than others. Contrary to common belief, it is not the weak-minded or impaired that are more susceptible to Hypnotism. It is instead, the open-minded and curious types.

1. <u>Motivation</u>. Remember how we talked about willing participants. If they have a problem, they are motivated to have a cure or coping mechanism. So, they look to Hypnotism as the road to that assist, and they are motivated to be hypnotized. People in hospitals or a clinical setting tend to be more motivated to be hypnotized than those in a home or work setting.

2. <u>Confidence</u>. The subject unwaveringly believes that they can be hypnotized. They have an unyielding self-confidence that Hypnotism is the solution, and they are susceptible. They are the people that are more prone to hypnosis than any other group.

3. <u>Patience</u>. You must have the patience to achieve this focused state of consciousness to zone in with tunnel vision on the task at hand. The mind tends to wander when sitting; still, that is natural, but you

must exhibit patience to teach your mind to stay in one place. This patience is a skill that can be learned if the participant is willing. If someone is highly-distracted by noises or voices, it can take a lot longer.

4. <u>Intelligence</u>. The higher the I.Q., the more likely the person is to be open to suggestion and hypnotized. I.Q. is correlated with performance in several tasks, and Hypnotism is no different. If the subject understands in the field of hypnosis and is well-versed, they tend to be more responsive to the process.

5. <u>Imagination</u>. Have you ever been reading a book and get so invested in it that you zone everything out? Or the latest drama series on T.V. and chaos could be going on around you, and you don't know it? This immersive behavior is the type of imagination that is more susceptible to hypnosis. The subject gets wholly immersed in daydreams, novels, or T.V. With this capability; they can zone into focused mode relatively easily.

Susceptibility to hypnosis and the experience is different for everyone. The key again is being open to the experience. If you are not a willing participant, then you are fighting any type of suggestion coming from anyone. So, technically, 100%

of the population could be hypnotized if they WANTED to be. It is beneficial to be able to look within for comfort and strength. Finding those attributes sometimes takes a calm, relaxed mind.

Different Types of Hypnotherapy

We have explored the history of Hypnotism, defined it, and identified what type of person is hypnotizable. It would be beneficial to mention different kinds of Hypnotherapy. Remember the history of psychology we discussed earlier (don't worry, I'm not good with dates either). We will call upon those founding fathers now to explain the types of Hypnotherapy used today.

Solution-Focused Hypnotherapy

Solution-Focused Hypnotherapy is the hypnotherapy method used by the majority of hypnotherapists. Solution-focused Hypnotherapy is just as it sounds. The Hypnotherapist and the client work together to find a solution instead of getting rid of the problem. This design is useful because it works towards something rather than trying to back up and remove a situation that may have been manifested for several years.

This type of Hypnotherapy focuses on the present. The Hypnotherapist keeps the client focused on where they are now and where they want to see themselves in the future. This type of therapy is client-centered, so the client decides where they want to go during these sessions and what the main objective is. Goal-setting is the plan, and the goals are defined by the Hypnotherapist asking leading questions to the client. The belief is that the client has the strength and self-conviction to draw upon their resources to become self-reliant.

Behavioral Hypnotherapy

Behavioral Hypnotherapy focuses on changing the behavior of the client. Hypnotherapy is useful in modifying future actions, which is particularly prevalent in eating disorders and smoking cessation, among other things. The Hypnotherapist works with the client to make a case history first to understand the behavior taking place before therapy begins. The client and Hypnotherapist then go over what behaviors the client finds unappealing or would like to change. The Hypnotherapist utilizes different techniques and hypnotic suggestions to 'plant' these behavioral modifications. The client wants to change these behaviors, and Hypnotherapy acts as a cohesive to help the client change them. As this Hypnotherapy is the least resistant by the client, it is usually the first approach used.

Cognitive Hypnotherapy

Unlike Behavioral Hypnotherapy, Cognitive Hypnotherapy focuses less on behaviors themselves and more on thoughts and beliefs that cause the behavior. This process rewires how a client thinks. The client may be thinking in ways that are not positive about themselves. Cognitive Hypnotherapy helps change the line of thinking and update the client's beliefs on a subconscious level. Cognitive Hypnotherapy pulls from several theories:

Cognitive Behavioral Therapy
Rational Emotive Behavior Therapy
Acceptance and Commitment Therapy

This list names just a few. The Hypnotherapist usually decides which approach they will incorporate after a client interview. The intake questions are analyzed, and the therapy is designed to match the client's goals and objectives. This type of treatment is incredibly successful with anxieties.

Analytical Hypnotherapy

This therapy is designed to find out why the client has a problem. The focus is to get to the root of the problem by finding out why you behave as you do. Hypnotherapists will work with the client to have that 'ah-ha' moment because the answer is usually stored within us, and we just didn't know it.

Ericksonian Hypnotherapy

Ericksonian Hypnotherapy is customized to the client. Ericksonian Hypnotherapy relies on the ability of the Hypnotherapist to read what kind of therapy the client needs. Ericksonian Hypnotherapy uses a combination of storytelling, metaphors, homework, indirect suggestions, and several other unique approaches to creating changes in the client, whether those changes be behavioral, cognitive, or analytical. It is comparable to the different learning styles that people have. Some need to see information to get the idea. Some need to hear it to understand. Some need to do it by having a hands-on experience. This Hypnotherapy works under the same premise using several different tools adapted to individual treatment.

Regression Hypnotherapy

Regression Hypnotherapy refers to taking a client through their mind. The Hypnotherapist walks the client to the past event that is the cause of their behavior. The exciting thing about Regression Hypnotherapy is that you can access both positive and negative events in a person's mind. This kind of therapy is used with great care and usually is reserved as a last resort because taking the client back to an adverse event could make them relive the event and re-traumatize the client.

If Regression Hypnotherapy is introduced as the first approach by a hypnotherapist, it is usually done if the client exhibits a phobia. There is an event that most likely triggered that phobia. Working within that triggering event will usually allow the phobia to be addressed and removed—exercise caution when a hypnotherapist recommends this as a first approach.

Past-Life Regression Hypnotherapy

As in Regression Hypnotherapy, Past-Life Hypnotherapy is for clients that believe in reincarnation and have an issue in a past-life. Some clients feel they have experienced memories of those past-lives and gain insight into their problems. Sometimes the goal is simply to disconnect from that life and the memories of that past life.

Hypnotherapists, in general, respect their client's beliefs. Some hypnotherapists believe past-life problems are a metaphor for change, while others believe in past-lives wholeheartedly. Still, others do not share the opinion but do not minimize the beliefs of their client and believe that there is a problem. Sometimes, it is hoped that memories discovered in Past-Life Regression Hypnotherapy will help answer why the client is struggling with issues in this life.

Clinical Hypnotherapy

Clinical Hypnotherapy is another way of saying Hypnotherapy performed in a clinical environment. It is the same Hypnotherapy that is practiced in an office setting. However, this Hypnotherapy is used to treat medical conditions such as pain, birth, psycho-sexual disorders, or skin problems. Clinical hypnotherapists focus in areas where other healthcare providers are still in charge of the care and management of the client's health portfolio.

Hypno-Psychotherapy

Hypno-Psychotherapy is the marriage of Hypnotherapy and psychotherapy. These therapists are dually trained in both areas of study. If they aren't, they should be. Some accelerated courses offer information in both areas but not full degrees for both disciplines. This type of therapy is used for more deep-seated issues and requires far more intensive work. Freud's theories that we talked about early come more into play here. This kind of therapy is where free association starts the room off with an even temperature. The back and forth puts the patient at ease and allows them to release their thoughts and maybe even a few Freudian slips along the way.

The Hypnotherapist can then latch on to that information and pull a few tidbits out of the subconscious in an attempt to analyze it and see where the problem is. Freud pulled suggestions out of psychoanalysis; however, the Hypnotherapist will find the appropriate docking station to suggest changing the behavior depending on what they see.

Psychotherapy refers to the back and forth from therapist to client. This conversational interaction helps with a broad array of mental illnesses and emotional issues. So, Hypno-Psychotherapy helps with a person to function better in society and increase their overall well-being. Deep-seated problems such as coping with daily life, impact trauma, death of a loved one, and mental disorders are the kind of 'big ticket' items that require a more in-depth look.

This in-depth look is why the Hypnotherapist should be skilled in both psychoanalysis and hypnosis. These Hypnotherapists are effectively combining both skills to the benefit of the patient. Hypno-Psychotherapy usually takes more time than other types of Hypnotherapy because it is unlikely to get results in one session. It will take several sessions for both the patient and the Hypnotherapist to find the root of the problem. Once the pattern has been established, then it can be treated.

Mindfulness

Although it is not a direct form of hypnosis, Mindfulness deserves an honorable mention. Mindfulness is a meditation that focuses attention on present moment awareness. You can see the similarity. Mindfulness can help you cope with stress but does take a significant amount of practice. The difference between hypnosis and Mindfulness is that hypnosis includes mental imagery and suggestions, while Mindfulness doesn't.

Mindfulness is considered to be an emotional regulator. There are five things to do to start practicing your mindful awareness.

1. <u>Wake Up Ready</u>. Wake up and get your mind in the game immediately. This momentum is known as 'setting your intention' for the day. Take deep refreshing breaths and take a moment to connect with your environment. Focus on what your mission is for the day and have it firmly centered in your mind. Visual possible obstacles and see yourself getting through them. Keep taking relaxing breaths for a few moments, demonstrating a calm before you get up and get ready for work.

2. <u>Enjoy Food</u>. Keep your senses aware of what you are doing. Breathe between bites and savor your food. Eat until your hunger subsides. Pay attention

to what your body tells you. Re-center yourself on your goal for the day before finishing up and going back to work. You should feel refreshed and not tired. Staying connected and in tune with what you do and how you do it is part of Mindfulness. This focused attention includes eating. Healthy mind, healthy body.

3. <u>Take A Minute</u>. It is said that 95% of what we do during the day is on autopilot. This autopilot nature leads to decreased awareness of everything around you and yourself as a whole. About every hour, take a minute to breathe and refocus on what is going on around you. You may see something that you overlooked before. If you are in a rut, try something new, like walking around when you are on a work call or taking a break to explore a part of the office you usually aren't in. Check-in with yourself frequently to make sure you absorb what is around you.

4. <u>WorkOut</u>. Working out is extremely helpful in clearing your head and reflecting on what has been going on around you. Working out for a half-hour a day will go a long way in helping you re-center and think through what you want your goals of the day to be. Quieting the mind is of paramount importance and a massive stress reliever.

5. <u>Stressfree Driving</u>. Before you start your car, take a few deep breaths and observe everything around you. Get the destination in your mind. Acknowledge the obstacles of heavy traffic and rude drivers, knowing that they will happen and how you will respond. Staying calm and connected with everything happening around you.

By breathing and practicing, how you will respond to things before they happen significantly improves your behaviors by keeping you calm. It also keeps you centered in the present with what may be happening around you. Mindfulness is an excellent tool to self-soothe before, during, and after stressful events.

Mindfulness is relatively new, and some hypnotherapists are beginning to incorporate the method with hypnosis. Most people that have been exposed to Mindfulness liked the ease of home practice. Mindfulness may start being seen more and more as a useful, therapeutic, self-soothing intervention. The ability for people to quickly learn how to do this, combined with the little amount of time and effort it takes to practice, makes Mindfulness an ideal method for everyday relaxation and reflection.

Common Uses of Hypnosis & Hypnotherapy

Hypnosis and Hypnotherapy have helped alleviate and treat a wide array of disorders and undesirable behaviors. For the people that participate, they will speak volumes about the healing that has taken place. Ancient cultures seemed to have known the benefits of the healing capabilities long before we did.

Hypnosis is used to treat pain, anxiety, phobias, stress, habit disorders, depression, gastrointestinal disorders, PTSD, weight problems, addictions, sleep, migraines, and several other conditions and behaviors. There is an unmeasurable amount of things that one human can have issues with, and nearly all of them can be helped with hypnosis if the person is a willing participant. The mind is a wondrous thing.

Myths of Hypnosis

Contradictions and misinformation surround hypnosis. It received a bad wrap in the 1990s when therapists convinced children that they were molested with no shred of evidence. During the McMartin Preschool Abuse Trial, the government spent seven years and $15 million investigating and prosecuting a case – with no convictions. Worse than that, hundreds of children were left emotionally scarred, and careers were ruined. Sadly, out of that trial, the Institute for Psychological Therapies -Forensics wrote:

"The interviews in the McMartin Preschool case illustrate how confusing the roles of therapist and investigator can result in leading and coercive questioning that creates memories for events that never happened. Therapy techniques have their roots in suggestion and social influence. Since hypnosis is best understood as a form of enhanced suggestibility, the research on hypnosis can be generalized to psychotherapy. Pavlov's research suggests that it is the healthiest individuals who are the most easily influenced. The combination of suggestibility to influence and obedience to authority means therapists must be very cautious about information elicited from clients in therapy. There is a difference between truth as dealt with in therapy and truth that involves others, particularly in the legal system."

The hoax was thrown to the side as research proved that you do not lose control of your mind when you are hypnotized, but it did not restore public faith in Hypnotherapy or hypnotherapists. The incident also damaged relationships between hypnotherapists and governmental authorities. Courts have primarily branded hypnotherapy sessions as inadmissible. Although the fiasco is long gone, it hurt the field of study considerably, and it has been a long road back. Below are some widely believed myths that it is time to debunk.

<u>Hypnotists Control Minds</u>. This myth is probably the biggest myth of them all. Stage show hypnotists are very different compared to Hypnotherapy in an office setting. It can not be said enough that you are in complete control of your mind. You are in a heightened state, knowing everything that is going on, and you are open to suggestion, but it doesn't mean that you have to agree with that suggestion. Your subconscious mind is capable of rejecting any proposal.

<u>Hypnosis is Black Magic & Not of This World</u>. That is entirely false. Since ancient times, hypnosis has been an altered state, even if we didn't recognize exactly why it occurred or explored it at the time as we have now. Hypnotherapy has been refined and examined over the last several hundreds of years through clinical research and well documented in Psychology and other areas of study.

<u>Hypnosis Is A Permanent State</u>. You cannot be permanently stuck in a hypnotic state. Hypnosis is safe and is a state of hyper-awareness. If you need to come out of it, you simply open your eyes, stretch or speak. It is similar to coming out of a dream. People enter this state at least twice a day without realizing it. Its that moment just before sleep or waking up.

Some enter hypnosis by merely being absorbed by a good movie or book.

Hypnosis is a Miracle Cure. As much as we would love that to be accurate, just to have a miracle cure-all, it is, in fact, false. Hypnosis can make a permanent improvement in a short amount of time, but there is no such thing as a one-time cure-all.

Summary

In this chapter, we covered the exciting history of hypnosis and Hypnotherapy. We also explored different kinds of Hypnotherapy and common traits of people that can be hypnotized. We also revealed the bumpy road that hypnosis has traveled at the hands of irresponsible therapists and the myths that have surrounded Hypnotism, some still alive and well today.

Hypnotism is a stable, reputable area of study, and its clients will sing praises for the healing powers that have been extended to them. It is a brilliant concept that we can heighten our senses if we silence the loud life around us. The mind is powerful, and there is no specific science or entity that fully understands all of its capabilities. So, why would it be so far-fetched that Hypnotism heals?

Mindfulness shows excellent promise in the psychological field as a way to self-soothe, stay calm, and be mindful of controlling emotions and thinking things through. Imagine how that would raise your emotional intelligence score.

Hypnosis as a therapy can be promoted for discouraging and alleviating several behaviors such as:

1. Eating disorders
2. Calming Anxiety & Paranoia
3. PTSD
4. Addictions
5. Child Birth
6. OCD
7. Grief
8. Sleep

And so many more. The possibilities are truly endless.

We also discussed the differences between hypnotic suggestion and subliminal messaging. They both speak to the unconscious but are very different in the modes of communication.

We discovered ways of reaching the unconscious and how those ways may provide insight into why we behave the way we do. Our subconscious is always beneath the service influencing us, even if we are unaware of it. Freud's theories proved various useful kinds of Hypnotherapy.

Scientists have yet to discover how clusters of neurons form in regions of our brain to develop consciousness. So, we may use all of our brains, but only understand about 10% of how it functions. Keeping an open mind and remaining curious are sure-fire ways to find something new.

Hypnosis is an ancient, time-tested, scientifically proven viable study and healing therapy. Saying that our mind is not capable of entering an intense state of focus is putting the cart before the horse. We have no idea what our minds are capable of of...yet.

114

CHAPTER 5: THE ART OF REVERSE & DARK PSYCHOLOGY

We have come full circle in the tool chest of Dark Psychology. We have arrived at Reverse Psychology. Reverse Psychology is utilized by many parents on children to get them to behave in a particular fashion. Reverse Psychology is used in nearly every relationship we have ever had. We see Reverse Psychology on the television, or mobile phones, and our computers. It runs rapidly throughout our society as a whole. In moderation, it is reasonably safe, and there is not an imbalance of power because it is so prevalent in the way we interact.

We spoke about hypnosis and its reliability on suggestion; Reverse Psychology works much the same way. It is a subtle suggestion in telling the other person how you would like them to behave while suggesting the opposite form of behavior. It appeals to the rebel in us of not like being told what to do. If someone says 'Don't do that,' the first thing we want to do is 'that.'

In simpler terms, Reverse Psychology is when you think the person will not do something that you want them to do, so you present it in a way that 'tricks' them into doing it. For example, you want your child to clean their room, but you want to avoid the 2-hour gut-wrenching fight that usually ensues when you ask them to do it. So, instead, you say something like, "I don't want your room cleaned today; it just creates laundry for me." In the act of telling them you DON'T want them to clean their room, you are suggesting that they *do* clean their room because you are implanting the idea in their head without actually asking them to do it with the bonus that it makes more work for you. Parents are masterful in the Reverse Psychology realm.

Reverse Psychology can be an excellent tool if used in moderation; however, there is a thin line in which it can cross over into a form of manipulation and damage a relationship. People do tend to get immune and annoyed if this is practiced on them too often. You probably use reverse psychology far more than what you think most people do. The interesting thing about Reverse Psychology is that it is only as good as the person using it. What that means is if you are apparent with your request, it is far less likely to influence someone to do your bidding; however, if you are incredibly crafty about it, you will have a higher success rate—the delivery matters. What also matters is the intent behind the action. After all, it is a form of manipulation, and it can quickly turn from semi-gray to dark.

Reactance in Reverse Psychology

Reverse Psychology doesn't work on everyone, no matter how well the delivery is by the user. There are two types of people, those that are compliant to Reverse Psychology and those that are resistant. Reactance plays a critical role in Reverse Psychology resistance. Reactance is the feeling that you get when someone tries to change a behavior or threaten freedom that you hold dear. Some people feel reactance by merely limiting their choices. People need to think that they are choosing items of their own free will, and minimizing that means you are taking freedom from them.

Let's say that you are about to eat a peanut butter and jelly sandwich. Your mom comes into the room and says, 'don't eat that.' You instantly want to eat it. You are a grown adult; you paid for the bread, the peanut butter, the jelly, the refrigerator, and the gas that took you to market to get it. You will be damned if someone is going to tell you not to eat that in your own house! What you may not know is your mom sees a club sandwich behind you on the counter that she wants to eat, and you haven't turned to see it yet. She is using your fierce independence against you to get what she wants. It's similar to someone saying 'Don't Push The Button,' well, now it's out there, and you simply have to push it, it's required.

The point being, if you show greater reactance, you are more likely to succumb to a Reverse Psychology trap. It should be noted that this tactic is used daily by car salesmen, lawyers, social media ads, and many other industries. It is particularly prevalent in all sorts of relationships.

How Reverse Psychology Is Used

Reverse Psychology is around you everywhere. If you think about it, even Disney deploys it in their movies. Aladdin tricked the Genie to lead him out of a cave by merely saying the Genie wasn't powerful enough to do it. Scar told Simba that only the bravest lions could go into the elephant graveyard in *The Lion King*. Movies seem harmless enough, right? After all, we saw that coming. But, there are other areas that Reverse Psychology is used that we may not even notice, at least not at first.

Reverse Psychology in Dating

Reverse Psychology is in great abundance in dating and intimate relationships. If someone starts giving you the cold shoulder, you feel an urgent need to do anything to get them to stop. Paying more attention to them, trying to find out what's wrong so you can fix it, while all along the person giving the cold shoulder wants you to be closer, so you are behaving how they want you to.

If you are continually chastising your partner about cheating, they are more likely to go out and cheat because you planted the idea in their head and kept reinforcing it. It goes the other way too, when an open-ended relationship is suggested, the partner indicated that sleeping with other women had lost its appeal because it wasn't forbidden.

If your partner does something undesirable or treats you poorly, withholding sex or affection is an effective form of reverse psychology to get them to treat you better. The breakdown here is that it is more satisfying to have something you had to work for than something that came quickly. As a result, Reverse Psychology is employed in every relationship, many times, without even realizing it. It becomes second nature.

You need to watch its overuse. Your partner will either get annoyed or act out because no one likes to be 'played.' If used in overabundance, it could disrupt the delicate balance of power and destroy the relationship by destroying the trust. How is your partner to trust you when you are saying things you don't mean? They will take on the defensive because you are trying to control their mind. This miscommunication is where it gets messy. Be aware of when and how you are using it in a relationship, preferably not at all, but it is hard to notice because we grew up with it as children, and reverse psychology is all around us in our daily lives.

Reverse Psychology in Advertising

When you see ads of 'Going Out of Business' you suddenly feel the need to go there. Several businesses indicate they are closing or going out of business to open up under 'New Management' with the same people. Advertising is designed to provide a sense of urgency to get you to act now. There are even advertisements cautioning you against buying this or buying that; anything that is forbidden (as we just learned) tastes better.

A great closer zones in on your reactance limit immediately. If they can see that you hate being told what is right for you, or what to do, you will find yourself in a new car in no time. Make that half the time if they tell you that you don't have what it takes to get that car, or to wear those jeans, or to try that workout juice. Reverse Psychology works best on people who fear change but have that competitive nature to be number 1.

You have seen it in action. People are prepping themselves before they even set foot on the car lot. The mantra going on in their head about how today is their day, they intend to outmaneuver the salesman and get that car for a lower price.

They carefully go over their leverage and recite all of the comebacks to the aggressive negotiations of the salesman. The mentality is an adversarial mode. Still, they go home with a car, usually not the car they set out to purchase and certainly not at the purchase price they set out to spend – but won because they still got a great deal. It's OK; it happens to the best of us.

Ads are so powerful that they teach reverse psychology and how to sell using it both in-person and on social media. Those ads you see are not worded that way by accident; it is by design. Those salesmen out there are students of sales pitch psychology. It's called Negative-Reverse Selling. Some of these tactics include:

1. <u>They do what you do</u>. When a salesperson mirrors you, he builds your trust. If he mimics your behavior, vibe, how you speak about things, and your posture, you will see him as more trustworthy, likable, and honest.

2. <u>Sell emotions, not logic</u>. More decisions are made based on emotion than logic, despite how logical we may seem. If a car reminds you of the 'good ole days,' the salesman will push that thought further into your head. Everyone wants to relive their youth. You will always be able to sell more on

emotions than by keeping someone focused clearly on facts.

3. <u>Fewer choices</u>. If you do not offer someone many choices, they will more than likely choose what you want them to, especially if you have been planting the idea in their head for the last hour. In this way, the buyer believes he had the choice when he didn't see all of the options.

4. <u>Ask Either/Or</u>. A salesman will always provide you with an either this or that scenario because it avoids answering 'No.' Do you want to see the Honda or the Ford? This choice limitation entices you to choose one option, which keeps the salesman in control of the situation.

5. <u>Fear of Missing Out</u>. This scarcity fear is used A LOT in today's marketplace. Providing a sense of urgency that indicates the sale won't be going on forever, or it's for a limited time, means that you might miss your chance. No one wants to miss out on their opportunity for a real deal. Some salesmen will even go so far as to take the price away to get you to say 'bring it back, I'm in.'

As discussed, these tactics should be used with care because an overabundance leads to distrust and disbelief. It won't work all of the time, and it won't work forever.

Reverse Psychology in Seduction

Psychology in seduction is separated from Reverse Psychology in Relationships because of the intent. Remember, we have discussed that intent is always something to be weighed and measured when you are on the receiving end of a message. Reverse Psychology in Seduction is taught on websites, mostly male frequented websites, worded something like "How To Get The Girl" or "Successful Dating With Women." These sites have millions of subscribers, and there are several thousands of books on the topic. So, the fact is, either you are one of 'those guys/girls' or you have been on the receiving end of the agenda for 'one of those guys/girls.'

That is not to be said that women are not predators; to the contrary, they most definitely are. The difference here is in intent. Women generally use the psychology of seduction towards a relationship. In contrast, the gentleman caller uses the psychology of seduction to a specific end and then aggressively backs away from any relationship.

For example, one website lists several different strategies of reverse psychology that work with women. Some are fun, like "Bringing Out the Naughty In Her," while others are not so fun, like "Predicting Miss Difficult." Now, before the ladies feel morally superior here, any issue of Cosmopolitan magazine offers articles on "How To Keep Your Man

Interested." The hard fact here is that consenting adults push & pull on seduction games to accomplish a means to an end, whether relationship-driven or one-night driven. Women practice this craft far more often than men; however, men simply talk about it more.

The Psychology behind Female Seduction is complicated because a woman tends to have a sexual-self to go along with her conscious self. Women do not think like men, and women tend to have an emotional element attached to most sexual encounters. Her head needs to be in the game to be turned on. Men are wired differently.

The moral of the story here is that no matter how pretty we want to paint the picture that we don't use seduction psychology, the absolute truth is, we do use it. These strategies go from playing it cool to saying you want to take it slow when you are close to taking your shirt off. Is it manipulation? You bet it is. But, remember there are levels of manipulation and intent. This dating genre generally is a fair playing field for both parties when first dating and getting to know each other.

That being said, if a relationship ensues, psychological seduction is something you want to watch if it is in overabundance because it could turn into full-on manipulation when there is an imbalance of power and the intent is to keep it that way.

Ethical Uses of Reverse Psychology

Some uses of Reverse Psychology are promoted as ethical. Not that the ones we have listed so far are unethical, it is natural in small doses and can evolve into dark manipulation. But, the below uses have been determined acceptable by a majority of the population.

What it comes down to, as always, is intent. If you are using reverse psychology to make a company perform better, it is considered a positive experience. If you are a personal trainer and are using it to have your client change their behavior in eating fatty foods, that is associated with a positive outcome.

Ethical reverse psychology means that you are in a better state after its application than before. Subsequently, unethical reverse psychology could be described as having regret after its application. This statement is, of course, an oversimplification, but if you look at intent and results, you know if it meets ethical by the way you feel about it.

How to Combat Reverse Psychology

We have discussed emotional intelligence and reading situations; this is always important. With reverse psychology, control over your emotions and keep calm and think things through while observing the intent behind what is being said helps to identify the motivation.

Reactance is the main ingredient for reverse psychology to take hold of. If you feel that your freedoms are being threatened, stop. Ask yourself, why do I think that my freedoms are being threatened? Do I want to do what this person is asking me to do? Or do I not want to do it at all? Having the ability to think through these situations will provide insight into whether you are being sucked into a reverse psychology activity.

Reverse psychology consumes our lives in several different mediums throughout the day, so becoming immune to it is easy; we simply don't think about it because it is always there. This fact makes identifying reverse psychology difficult. If you feel defensive when someone is asking you to do something, that is a sign that you may be a willing victim. The best thing that you can do is recognize this feeling and take a breath before you proceed. Find the understanding of why you feel that way and what the intent of the conversation is. If you can pinpoint that, you can flip the script and not succumb to reverse psychology. Freedom of choice, true freedom, not suggested, is the best defense.

Summary

Reverse psychology is used in everyday life by many parents, social media, and ads on the television. We discussed the signs and how to combat reverse psychology if someone is using it on you. Everything is good in moderation is a common saying – the same holds true of reverse psychology. Therapists limit its use because it can be destructive if used too much.

Knowing how it is used in dating games and relationships is of paramount importance to maintain the balance of power. One person in a relationship should never have all of the power in a relationship. If you feel that there is an imbalance, brush up on your awareness of the situation through Mindfulness and in the practice of emotional intelligence skills.

Throughout this book, you should have started seeing a common trend developing:

1. Attempt to discover the intent of the message
2. Be aware of your surroundings

3. Be aware of your emotions

4. Keep your emotions under control demonstrate emotional intelligence

5. Read the situation, body language, tones, etc.

6. React with thought, take a breath if you need

If you practice these with every conversation and relationship, you are less likely to fall victim to ploys of manipulation. Keeping circumstances in your control may require you to make behavioral changes. These behavioral changes can be hard to do, but if you keep your eye on the goal of success in self-worth, family, career, community (and the money too), you will live a far more satisfying life.

Elevating yourself does not mean putting down or degrading other people. It means setting clear and concise boundaries for yourself and having the strong convictions to relay that communication of acceptable behaviors to others and encourage others through positive reinforcement. By bringing out your best self, you promote people to be their best selves, and it is contagious.

There are times when you will hit life lows; we all do. Your mind may become exhausted, especially at times with massive life shifts, like changing careers, moving for a new job, or even the loss of a loved one. If you are not in your prime state of mind and looking for easy answers, another lethal predator is waiting in the wings that you may fall victim to if you are not alert enough due to the preoccupation with changes in your life. This predator uses mind control.

CHAPTER 6: BRAINWASHING

When you think of brainwashing, you probably think of movies like "A Clockwork Orange," which was a dystopian film with violent images of psychiatry, delinquency, young gangs waging both social and political warfare. Or, you may think of something a little more recently, such as the Divergent Trilogy or even the Hunger Games Trilogy. All of these movies have an element of brainwashing.

One particular instance in the "Hunger Games" was when Peeta was kidnapped by the Capitol and put through torture and reward, to condition him to hate his best friend and love interest, Katniss. When Katniss sent a team in to rescue Peeta, it was all too easy for them to get in and save him. The reason, the second he was alone with Katniss, he tried to kill her. The brainwashing that the Capitol applied to Peeta was successful with many emotionally damaging side effects. It would take Peeta years to retrain his brain and combat the mind control, and the threat was never fully extinguished that he would kill Katniss. It changed him, and he was no longer who he used to be. That person was gone forever.

Brainwashing is extraordinarily invasive and damaging, with long-term effects that are never entirely undone. The term brainwashing goes back to the Cold War that took place in the 1950s. Professor Daniel Pick coined the phrase in speaking about the mind control used on prisoners of war on both sides. Fears of brainwashing and mind control ran rapid in American's minds, scared that Communists were taking over through deceptive mind control strategies.

Brainwashing was defined as changing someone's thoughts and beliefs against their will. This fear was fed when 5,000 of the 7,200 prisoners of war petitioned the U.S. to end the war or signed confessions of crimes they didn't commit. The height of brainwashing panic ensued when 21 American soldiers refused repatriation.

In 1953, Allen Dulles was the new Director for the CIA. The CIA was just in its infancy, but with the fear of brainwashing in mainstream culture and America on edge and untrusting, Dulles had a plan to get to the bottom of things. In his quote:

"In the past few years, we have become accustomed to hearing much about the battle for men's minds—the war of ideologies. I wonder, however, whether we perceive the magnitude of the problem, whether we realize how sinister the battle for men's minds has become in Soviet hands. We might call it, in its new form, 'brain warfare.'"

And so began several atrocities in the CIA in testing brainwashing techniques and exploring the topics of mind control and the hysteria of the American people both intrigued and highly disturbed about the phenomenon.

MK-Ultra

A few days after that speech, Dulles approved MK-Ultra. The program was designed to study the use of chemical and biological warfare combined with mind control tactics. The study was focused on changing behavior through electro-shock therapy, polygraphs, radiation, hypnosis coupled with a massive amount of different kinds of drugs and toxins.

The test subjects were comprised of volunteers (some free, some coerced); some had no idea they were in an experiment, mentally-impaired boys at state schools, American soldiers, and sexual psychopaths at a state hospital. The CIA especially loved the use of prisoners in these experiments.

One of the drugs the CIA used was LSD. If you have ever seen the movie Jacobs Ladder, it refers to the testing of LSD on veterans. Whitney Bulger, one of the prisoners that were injected with LSD, said:

"Eight convicts in a panic and paranoid state," Bulger said of the 1957 tests at the Atlanta penitentiary where he was serving time. "Total loss of appetite. Hallucinating. The room would change shape. Hours of paranoia and feeling violent. We experienced horrible periods of living nightmares and even blood coming out of the walls. Guys turning to skeletons in front of me. I saw a camera change into the head of a dog. I felt like I was going insane."

This experience left hundreds of people emotionally scarred for life, and hallucinations never entirely stopped. The CIA knew it was engaging in unethical behavior and documented that it needs to be hidden from the American public. They entertained LSD as an 'offensive' drug that would allow them to take control of other people's bodies, willing or not.

Operation Midnight Climax

The CIA was so confident in this ability that they would slip it into other CIA agents' drinks to see what would happen. George White was an FBI agent in narcotics. The CIA thought it would be a good idea to bring him into their next big experiment, Operation Midnight Climax. He decorated a room in provocative, sexually evoking paraphilia as a trap. They promptly had the room bugged and installed a two-way mirror. George White took his martini and sat on one side of the two-way mirror, while a prostitute he hired lured the men into 'room erotica and dosed them with LSD.

White became infatuated with the sex that took place there, and the room became known as the 'CIA Carnal House.' Agents began to see that they could elicit confessions best after sex. So, they discussed bringing prostitutes in as informants and the possibility of how prostitutes would handle state information. It became clear that White may have lost plot when he said this:

"I toiled wholeheartedly in the vineyards because it was fun, fun, fun. Where else could a red-blooded American boy lie, kill, cheat, steal, rape, and pillage with the sanction and blessing of the All-Highest?"

Patty Hearst

Probably one of the more famous stories is that of Patty Hearst. She was kidnapped in the 1970s and believed brainwashed into committing crimes. Patty's kidnappers were radicals known as the Symbionese Liberation Army (SLA). They were led by a criminal named Donald DeFreeze and looked to incite warfare in the U.S. and destroy capitalism. Patty was 19 years old at the time of her kidnapping.

Patty was a significant capture from a wealthy family. Her grandfather was William Randolph Hearst. The SLA was correct; America was stunned. So, they asked for food donations worth millions for her release while they abused her and brainwashed her into becoming the poster child for their cause.

A few months later, the SLA released a video with Patty obediently saying that she had joined them. About two weeks later, she was caught on surveillance cameras holding an assault weapon and robbing a bank with the SLA. America's fear of brainwashing renewed.

You may think that brainwashing only happens in the movies or extreme cases such as in POW camps. Unfortunately, it is more common than you think, and anyone can fall victim to it.

How Brainwashing Happens

The stories are disturbing, especially since they are real. It is not some far off land that brainwashing takes place; it is right here at home. Some of the more horrific brainwashings take place in authoritative entities.

If it doesn't bother you, it should. Brainwashing destroys people's lives. The victim, the people around them, and deep-seated faith in the good of humanity gets shaken taken years to unravel. After reading those stories, you are left with the 'How could someone do that?' question. You are simultaneously convincing yourself that 'I would never do that.' Are you so sure?

During World War II, Hitler's Youth Program used propaganda and brainwashing techniques to form the youth into an ideal soldier for the Nazi agenda. By forcing his values into young minds, Hitler was attempting to secure his future and eliminate opposition. Hitler's influence was strong in several countries. So, how did he do that? Through brainwashing and thought reform. Thought reform was prevalent in several different countries' prison camps and resembled what happened with Patty Hearst. Turn opposers into soldiers, very much like Peeta in the "Hunger Games," just without the physical torture.

Thought Reform

Brainwashing is often thought of as thought reform. Thought reform relies on social influence. We have discussed how social influence enters your life every minute of every day. There is a vast collection of ways to influence behavior this way. Brainwashing is an amplified use of all of the persuasion and manipulation techniques delivered with propaganda. It is an incredibly severe form of social influence to change a person's mind through coercion, entirely without consent.

Brainwashing requires an invasive strategy and isolation, making prison camps an ideal structure for it. However, cults also offer a grand stage in which to trap a mind. Full control is exercised over the victim. When they sleep, eat, go to the bathroom, and basically, every primary need is up to the one doing the brainwashing. The goal is to break the victim down until broken completely. Then the brainwasher builds them back up with another set of behaviors and beliefs better structured around the list of the brainwasher.

How Brainwashing Is Done

In the 1950s, Robert Jay Lifton, a psychologist, studied the POWs formerly in Korean and Chinese war camps. Lifton defined these steps as to how to brainwash someone:

1. Assaulting Their Identity. *You aren't who you think.* The powers that be break this person down, so the victim loses all convictions of who they are. They doubt themselves. Maybe I'm not a teacher or a soldier. They begin to lose the sense of what they were about as an individual.

2. Guilt. *You are bad.* The victim is criticized for all of their beliefs and weaknesses. All of their 'evil' deeds are showcased in front of them. Creating an overwhelming sense of guilt for everything the victim stood for simultaneously is being assaulted for who they thought they were.

3. Self-betrayal. *Agreeing that you are evil.* With the victim losing their sense of identity and feeling the guilt and remorse being pushed upon them, they start to agree that they may be wrong after all. This agreement is usually done under the threat of physical violence.

4. Breaking Point. *Who am I? Where am I? What am I supposed to do?* This questioning of oneself is where the victim succumbs to the deep sense of shame and often goes into a depression with manic crying fits. They feel like they are losing their grip on reality because of their lost identity. The victim has lost their belief system and structure of the self, so it is an ideal time for the brainwasher to start suggesting the belief structure that they want to see.

5. Granting Leniency. *I can help you.* The brainwasher offers the victim some small token of leniency, a relief. The victim is spiraled into an appreciation for the kindness as they grasp at straws trying to figure out who they are.

6. Compulsion to Confess. *You can help yourself.* The brainwasher empowers the victim with the ability to control their surroundings and seek absolution through confession. The victim will feel the need to reciprocate the kindness afforded them in the leniency, resulting in the admission.

7. Channeling of Guilt. *This evil is why you're in pain.* After being assaulted for endless weeks or months, the victim just knows that they are wrong. They are not sure why they are wrong anymore; they just are. They need redemption. At this point, the brainwasher can implant the full belief structure that they would like to see. The victim recognizes he is wrong and is more than ready to be right.

8. Releasing Guilt. *It's not me; it's my beliefs.* Since it isn't the victim that's bad, it's just his old belief structure. The victim is relieved that he can toss the wrong belief structure aside and get into the right system of beliefs to make all of this hurt and guilt go away. The victim's full confession is the rejection of their old identity and the taking on the new one. The pain stops.

9. Progress and Harmony. *If you want, you can choose the right.* The brainwasher completely stops the abuse and steps in a nurturer and calming agent. They are offering encouragement and praise. The victim feels

the comfort and the absence of pain, the victim, is empowered to choose his path. The choice isn't hard. The victim has already surrendered their former identity and replaced it with the new structure. The victim was in pain before and isn't now. They instantly see the relief and reflect, saying this is the right path, and I choose it.

10. Final Confession and Rebirth. *I choose good.* When the victim decides the 'good,' they hang onto it with ferocity because their once painful, tormented life is now peaceful and serene. They don't want the old experience they had, which they remember in flashbacks of torment.

There are various tools used to achieve each step in this process, including the threat of physical harm, sleep deprivation, malnutrition, and mind-clouding. With all of these things in play, it is challenging to keep an independent thought because you are so overwhelmed with your basic needs. When it is broken down in steps, you see what kind of permanent scar this puts on a victim.

Mental Detachment is now one of the POW survival techniques taught to soldiers. The soldier learns how to remove themselves from their surroundings to avoid brainwashing psychologically. Kind of like putting your identity in a safebox and opening it three times a day to remember who you are and then putting it back into your mind for safekeeping. Soldiers are also taught about brainwashing techniques because if you understand what is going on, you will be less susceptible to it. Just by reading this chapter, you are a bit less susceptible. Certain personality traits make brainwashing more effective.

Traits in a Brainwashing Victim

It has been said that **anyone** can be at a vulnerable stage when dealing with a loss, or feeling like their life isn't making sense and open themselves up for manipulation and mind-control. Sadly, that is quite correct. If you are not on your 'A' game and someone says they see you are unique and know how to get you to your goals, you might lend an ear, and the next thing you know, you are in a situation and have no idea how you got there. It happens to the best of us every single day.

We are humans, and as such, we become emotionally vulnerable from time to time. Other personality traits are also believed to play a part in how easily allow brainwashing to invade your life in one form or another:

1. If you suffered abuse or neglect as a child
2. Commonly experience self-doubt & self-loathing

3. Have a weak sense of identity& low self-confidence
4. Show a sense of guilt of who you are or what you've done
5. High level of stress
6. Dissatisfaction with your life
7. Desire to belong to a group
8. Naïve or gullible, cultural disillusionment
9. Frustrated spiritually

You are confronted with manipulation every day; we have established that. Brainwashing is manipulation on steroids, and anyone can easily fall victim to it if they are having an off day or a bit lost in their path at the moment; we have all been there.

Looking at victim traits, you can see how all of us have felt these things at some point in our life. Focused preying on circumstance is why brainwashing is extraordinarily dangerous and presents itself as an ideal solution if someone has the answers that we are seeking and any one time in our lives. You have to have the strength to know that you will get through it without the assistance of a newcomer that has all of the answers. Would you believe that Scientology is considered a cult?

Cults and Brainwashing

If you think that cults are a thing of the past, think again. There are nearly 2.5 million people in cults today. Not all cults are dangerous; a lot of them are harmless. The intent and morality of a cult are dependent on the leader. However, you need to decipher what kind of cult you may be in; yes, you could be in a cult without even realizing it. It is not the weak-minded that get pulled into groups they shouldn't be. As we discussed, people usually arrive in a cult by accident on an emotionally vulnerable day.

A cult shares an unyielding commitment to a leader or the leader's ideology. The cult generally has an answer to all life's questions and the solutions. High levels of commitment are required from its members. There are four qualities that you will see in any cult.

1. Charismatic Leader.
2. Transcendent Belief System
3. Systems of Control; and
4. Systems of Influence

The leader always plays a critical role in a cult. Several studies have been done indicating that cult leaders have Narcissistic personality disorder. They need adoration, a sense of entitlement, do not care about other's feelings. Emotional intelligence would play a key role in attempting to decipher the intent of leaders of this caliber.

There are a variety of cults; again, not all of them are bad. Eastern cults typically mediate and explore altered states of consciousness. New Age cults are into tarot cards, exploring chakras and looking inside of one-self to self-soothe. Cults can be extremely dangerous on many levels; there are a few you may know.

The Peoples Temple

The People's Temple was a charitable organization that provided a free medical clinic incorporated with a drug rehabilitation program. At least, that is how it started. It ended with over 900 lives in a mass suicide in 1978. Reverend James Warren Jones was the leader. It appeared that he began abusing prescription drugs and was getting more and more paranoid. He had moved his sect to Guyana and without much outside influence, and in keeping his people isolated, he was able to exploit them at will and feed into his paranoia. A Congressman visited the sect with three journalists who were shot after too many questions erupted. After the shooting, Jones convinced his followers to kill themselves with poisoned flavor aid, including the children who drank first.

The Branch Davidian

David Koresh started the Branch Davidian. He had been banished from the Seventh-day Adventist Church for preaching his unconventional ideas to the youth. Many followers left with him. In 1993, the FBI raided their compound in Waco, Texas, leaving 76 dead. The followers believed in an imminent apocalypse.

The Manson Family

Charles Manson has a highly disturbed, narcissist, yet charismatic personality. He was a musician who learned to play the guitar in prison. He had a desert commune and about 100 followers in the 1960s. The lifestyle consisted of hallucinogenic drugs and the belief that a race war would occur in 1969, and the commune would rule the world after it. When that didn't come to fruition, he sent his followers on a murder spree to get the war going, but the victims Manson chose were those that failed to help him with his music career.

Cults offer a sense of belonging, they accept you for your worst and your best – at least that is how you feel, and it's what you want to feel when you are down on life at a particular time. It's slow, methodical acceptance that gets you—the feeling of family when you need it most.

There are several different types of cults, again, not all of them bad. Some, such as Doomsday cults, are incredibly evil and tend to lead to the death of members for some greater belief that the world is coming to an end, and the only way to transcend is to die.

Signs of Dangerous Cults

A cult is nothing more than a social group whose beliefs are not in line with mainstream beliefs. This difference is usually referring to unusual religious or philosophical ideas that are outside of societal norms or goals.

Cults that pose a danger have these following characteristics:

1. The leader has all of the control; it is not a democracy
2. There is no questioning the leader; his orders are absolute
3. Members will not be privy to any financial disclosures
4. There is fear for the outside world and some pending catastrophe or conspiracy
5. If you leave the cult, you are evil
6. Former members discuss abuse from the cult
7. There are recorded documents or allegations surrounding accusations of abuse within the cult

8. Followers are never good enough and need to keep trying

9. No one but the leader is a credible source

There is a recent indication that there is a Doomsday cult using Coronavirus for recruiting new members. Dangerous cults are still around today. Steve Hassan, a cult expert, said: "Cult leaders always know that when there's a major disruption if there's an economic problem if there's a terrorist attack if there's an earthquake or tsunami, they're going to capitalize on that because they use fear as a primary manipulation tool to make people feel like it's not safe out there."

When there is an opportunity, people are always there in a predatory mode to take advantage of the situation. This is particularly true in the case of cults. They gain membership through fear and offering the cure or solution for that fear.

Doomsday cults believe in apocalypticism and millenarianism. They feel they know how to predict disaster. They also think they can see those that intend to destroy the entire universe. Doomsday cults are more then 'Debbie Downers'; they usually involve a deadline for ritualistic suicides if the leadership goes south. Cults as the whole depend on their leader. When leadership unravels, the entire cult structure unravels unless another charismatic leader takes on the responsibility and is accepted by the membership.

Be wary of these characteristics in any organization. Dangerous cults are a relevant topic to be aware of and look out for. If you see many similarities, it is time to back out of the situation.

Brainwashing in Relationships

Brainwashing doesn't always happen outside the home. It can happen inside your home. We have covered dark manipulations and covert manipulation, this kind of manipulation is incredibly dark and insidious. This brainwashing comes from someone that you love. The same techniques used in manipulation are applied to brainwashing when you are in a relationship—tearing you down, building you back up to think the way the brainwasher wants you to believe. Because it is happening in your home, you may not see that it is brainwashing, and odds are you are isolated so that you wouldn't have any outside perspective telling you otherwise.

The perpetrator keeps you under control as you lose your sense of identity. The heightened sense of anxiety you feel prevents you from thinking clearly about what is happening. The brainwashing sneaks upon you, and you don't often recognize the imbalance of power.

We have discussed how cult leaders have narcissist personalities. If your partner shows the signs of being a narcissist, there is cause for concern. The techniques that they use in manipulation transfer efficiently into the brainwashing techniques that we discussed above. Often, these are abusive relationships, and you need help getting out. Sandra Brown, M.A., indicated that these women were more susceptible to an abusive relationship:

- perfectionists
- hold themselves to high standards
- persistent
- resourceful
- goal-directed
- self-sacrificing
- previous victims of abuse or neglect
- experience dependence, vulnerability, or incompetency issues

If you feel that you are not living your own life, it is time to examine the relationship and start practicing on increasing your emotional intelligence to gain perspective on the situation.

Summary

Brainwashing is an incredibly volatile and destructive form of manipulation. Reprogramming people requires insurmountable mistreatment that lasts for years and is not easily 'removed' after the psyche has been this damaged. Sadly, the charismatic leader is easy to like, offers solutions for your problems, and it happens at a head-spinning pace.

The kind of brainwashing that took place in POW camps may seem extreme, but it can happen just as quickly in your own home. Tearing a person down to a nub, taking their identity, and rebuilding them in your image is painstakingly cruel.

There is no more significant violation of someone than ripping them down and making them live in anxiety for any amount of time. People are capable of atrocious acts that can seem normal if the normal is stripped away, and you have nothing to compare it to. The Mob used similar techniques of family and threats of violence. Would you consider them a cult?

The best defense against brainwashing is always asking yourself why. It is vital to look at intent and determine the motive for what you are being asked to do. If you are off your game due to a significant life event, know that you have the inner strength to get through it. Lean on those in your life that you trust for emotional support. If an outsider comes in with all of the solutions to your problems, be wary. No one has the answer to life's questions; there are no immediate fixes. We go through pain to appreciate what we have and learn where we are going.

Each challenge in your life should be recognized as there is something worth getting to on the other side. So, challenges are treasure maps. You need to overcome them to find a higher purpose or reach a goal. Pain is a necessary evil, so we know appreciation and gratitude. In matters of the heart, there is no easy course, so you must be able to reach into yourself, confident in the tools you have learned here, that you have what it takes to get through this and any other situation.

CONCLUSION

The world is full of things that are beyond your control. You can't control how people behave. You can't force them to be better people, although you can certainly set an example. The point is, what you can control is how prepared you are. That translates to anything you do, not just the dark forces at large.

You study before an exam; you practice driving, you read the instructions before settling in with a glass of wine to put your new Ikea desk together. You prepare so you can succeed. You gain the knowledge that you need to achieve the goal and the outcome that you want. You are exercising your control over things that you have control of.

By reading this book, you know more about what is lurking out there, and you know more about how to handle it. Being able to practice and grow your emotional intelligence skills will assist you in creating healthy connections with people. Setting proper boundaries will assist in keeping predators at bay. By no means should you take on the mantra of 'I don't trust anyone'; however, you should exercise caution and be an astute observer of people, especially when getting to know them.

Paying close attention to conversations, body language, and tones will help you decipher the intent. Trust your instincts; if you feel in your gut that something is wrong, it probably is. Be aware of your feelings and why you are feeling them. That is going to serve as your main red flag. How you think, why do you feel that way – those are two questions that you should be asking yourself.

No one can live in a bubble; humans are social creatures and need interaction. The purpose of this book was to prepare you to handle those interactions better to avoid people and predators with destructive behaviors that will throw your life path off course. It is far easier to avoid an abusive relationship than it is to pick up the pieces after.

If you were unable to avoid the relationship, we have given you the steps to help you heal and rebuild. Outside help is always recommended to guide you through repairing your self-confidence and self-worth. Abusive relationships can make you feel lost, unworthy, and overwhelmed with how to start over. Outside help would be an excellent guide to start you going. After every hardship is a more robust, better-informed survivor. Know in your heart that you are one.

Prepare yourself for the bad things in life but expect the good to come your way. That's all that optimism is. Being prepared and knowledgeable, being sure of who you are, and believing in yourself is all you need. You have friends because you want them, not because you need them. There is a difference. Lead by example; it is contagious and will positively affect you and those around you. Love yourself; it is the key to true happiness.

www.ingramcontent.com/pod-product-compliance
Lightning Source LLC
Chambersburg PA
CBHW061805250726
48657CB00001B/294